The private life of palaces
Fifteen stories from five amazing palaces
Julian Humphrys

Historic Royal Palaces is
the charity that looks after:

Tower of London

Hampton Court Palace

Banqueting House

Kensington Palace

Kew Palace

Hillsborough Castle

We help everyone explore
the story of how monarchs
and people have shaped
society, in some of the
greatest palaces ever built

We raise all our own funds
and depend on the
support of our visitors,
members, donors,
sponsors and volunteers.

Contents

Welcome to Historic Royal Palaces_____I
Five extraordinary palaces_____II
How you can help us keep the stories alive_____IV

1. Colonel Blood and the Crown Jewels_____07
2. The most famous maze in the history of the world_____13
3. 'May you never die a Yeoman Warder'_____19
4. 'As mechanical as the clock'_____21
5. The first London zoo_____27
6. A taste of palace history_____33
7. A poignant place of execution_____35
8. 'I will be good'_____41
9. 'The finest and most artistic in England'_____47
10. Feeding the twelve hundred_____53
11. 'The simplest country gentlefolks'_____57
12. 'Fortifications which the French call castles'_____65
13. Everything but the ghost_____71
14. 'Dispatch me quickly'_____73
15. A job not to be sneezed at_____79

Acknowledgements_____80

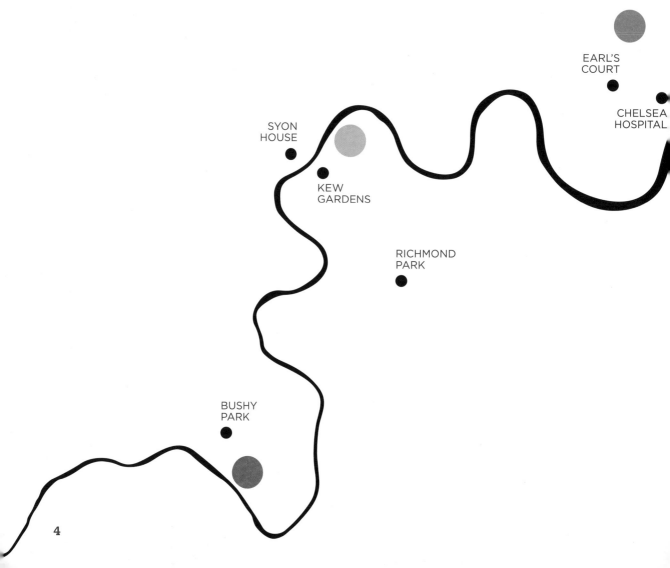

EARL'S
COURT

CHELSEA
HOSPITAL

SYON
HOUSE

KEW
GARDENS

RICHMOND
PARK

BUSHY
PARK

Welcome to Historic Royal Palaces

In a world that is more uncertain than ever, people are searching for roots, foundations and anchors. They want to understand how the past shaped the present, and they want to protect the things they value. In this respect, I believe that we at Historic Royal Palaces have a unique role to play.

We look after five extraordinary places; each with its own character, all symbolic of Britain. We care for these places; we investigate them, learn about them, repair, conserve and restore them. We welcome visitors and stage events: indeed, we have a tradition of putting on a great show. And they are not just places but palaces, where monarchs and their courts have lived, and where history was made. These palaces witnessed many of the defining moments that collectively explain our nation's history.

Our challenge is to help everyone explore the story of how monarchs and people have shaped society in some of the greatest palaces ever built. As you will discover from this book, each of the palaces has its own story to tell: the Tower of London, a place of ancient power, incarceration and execution; the majestic Hampton Court Palace, famous for Henry VIII's romances and fabulous entertainments; the Banqueting House, a landmark to the rise and fall of the monarchy; stylish Kensington Palace, where the young Princess Victoria learned that she was to be queen; and Kew Palace, where George III and his family enjoyed a comparatively simple and happy domestic life until illness shadowed their lives.

This book reveals many of the untold stories that are part of the fabric of each palace. In turn it will help you explore your own story, which we know will give an added dimension to your visits.

If you haven't already decided to become a member of Historic Royal Palaces, we hope you will soon do so. As a valued member, you will enjoy a range of benefits, not least free entry to all of our palaces for the duration of your membership. You will also receive regular newsletters that will tell you about life at Historic Royal Palaces: conservation projects, exhibition openings, events which help explain our stories even more vividly, education and learning opportunities for all ages and much more. I hope that you will become a regular visitor to Historic Royal Palaces and support our work over the years to come.

Michael Day, Chief Executive

Five extraordinary palaces

The Tower of London
The ancient stones reverberate with dark secrets, priceless jewels glint in fortified vaults and ravens strut the grounds. The Tower of London, founded by William the Conqueror in 1066-7, is one of the world's most famous fortresses, and one of Britain's most visited historic sites. Despite a grim reputation as a place of torture and death, there are so many more stories to be told about the Tower. This powerful and enduring symbol of the Norman Conquest has been enjoyed as a royal palace, served as an armoury, public record office and can even lay claim to being the original London Zoo! An intriguing cast of characters have played their part: including the jewel-thief Colonel Blood, tragic Lady Jane Grey and maverick zoo-keeper Alfred Cops.

Hampton Court Palace
The flamboyant Henry VIII is most associated with this majestic palace, which he extended and developed in grand style after acquiring it from Cardinal Wolsey in the 1520s. He lavished money on fabulous tapestries and paintings, housed and fed a huge court and pursued political power and domination over Rome. The Tudor buildings that remain are among the most important in existence, but the elegance and romance of the palace owes much to the baroque buildings commissioned by William and Mary at the end of the 17th century. The palace is set in 60 acres of gardens, which include the famous Maze and Great Vine.

The Banqueting House, Whitehall
This revolutionary building, the first in England to be designed in a Palladian style by Inigo Jones, was finished in 1622 for James I. Intended for the splendour and exuberance of court masques, the Banqueting House is probably most famous for one real life drama: the execution of Charles I which took place here in 1649 to the 'dismal, universal groan' of the crowd. One of the King's last sights as he walked through the Banqueting House to his death was the magnificent ceiling, painted by Peter Paul Rubens in 1630-4.

Kensington Palace

The feminine influence of generations of royal women has shaped this stylish palace and elegant gardens. The birthplace and childhood home of Queen Victoria, the palace first became a royal residence for William and Mary in 1689. Mary felt 'shut in' at Whitehall and much preferred her new Kensington home, which was enlarged by Sir Christopher Wren. In the 18th century, the famous Orangery was built for Queen Anne, while the interior of the palace was lavishly remodelled and decorated for George I. George II's wife, Queen Caroline, made further improvements to the gardens. Today, the palace houses a stunning permanent display of fashionable and formal dresses, the Royal Ceremonial Dress Collection, which includes dresses worn by Her Majesty The Queen and Diana, Princess of Wales.

Kew Palace and Queen Charlotte's Cottage

The most intimate of the five royal palaces, Kew was built as a private house in 1631 and used by the royal family between 1729 and 1818, in conjunction with several other buildings nearby which no longer exist. At various times, George III, Queen Charlotte and some of their 15 children enjoyed a relatively rural domestic routine at Kew. The palace rang with laughter and fun as family games and birthday celebrations provided the distractions from affairs of state. However, in later years family rivalries became more intense and relationships soured. Kew became a retreat for an ailing King George and a virtual prison for his elder unmarried daughters. The nearby Queen Charlotte's Cottage is also managed by Historic Royal Palaces. It was built in 1770, and later enlarged and decorated as a cottage *orné*.

How you can help us keep the stories alive

Did you know that you can make a valuable contribution to the care, conservation and public presentation of the palaces in our care?

Historic Royal Palaces was established in 1998 as a Royal Charter Body with charitable status and is contracted by the Secretary of State for Culture, Media and Sport to manage the palaces on her behalf. We do not receive any funding from Government or the Crown but rely on generating income from visitor ticket sales, retail and catering outlets and the sensitive commercial exploitation of our sites for conferences, receptions and other events.

We also fundraise to enable us to embark on new conservation and restoration projects and to broaden and develop additional programmes of education and learning. Recent projects have included the Tower Environs Scheme which has created one of the largest open spaces in the City of London and opened up the views of the Tower and its grounds; the restoration and re-presentation of Kew Palace, the former home of George III and his family; two internships in our Textile Conservation Studio; a variety of community programmes involving disabled and other groups, and the restoration of the Long Water at Hampton Court Palace.

Our job is to give these palaces a future as valuable as their past. We know how precious they and their contents are and we aim to conserve them to the standard they deserve: the best. You can help us by:
- becoming a member of Historic Royal Palaces – remember that membership gives free access to each of the palaces for the duration of your membership
- encouraging friends and family to join – or giving membership to them as a gift
- becoming a volunteer
- becoming a patron of Historic Royal Palaces
- making a donation, either in support of a specific project or more generally for the conservation and education work we undertake – this can be a cash gift, a gift of shares or land
- leaving us a legacy.

If you are a UK tax payer, you can increase the value of your donation through the UK Government Gift Aid Scheme at no additional cost to yourself. You simply declare that you are a UK tax payer, confirming that you have paid Income/Capital Gains Tax at least equal to the tax on your donation, and that you would like to Gift Aid your donation whilst providing us with your full name and address.

More about membership

History is never just about the past. It's about how yesterday helped shape today. It's about how we came to be who we are. It's about a story that belongs to all of us, one you can discover for yourself with a Historic Royal Palaces membership.

Joining Historic Royal Palaces is the perfect way to explore the inside story of five extraordinary places that helped define our nation's history. What's more, you'll save money and contribute to the important work of conserving the palaces at the same time.

Membership of Historic Royal Palaces means the freedom to visit the Tower of London, Hampton Court Palace, the Banqueting House, Kensington Palace and Kew Palace as often as you like. Discover the story of kings and queens, politicians and servants, rogues and rebels, craftsmen and traders, philosophers and philanderers, guards and gardeners. It's all here, waiting to be discovered. Membership also means you don't have to queue – simply walk in to see, experience and understand what made us who we are.

Every penny of your subscription helps maintain these marvellous palaces. Our *Inside Story* newsletter is packed with information about the vital conservation work your money will support, along with news about forthcoming events and exhibitions, life at the palaces and the colourful characters and fascinating stories that make them part of our national heritage. If you've ever wanted to get closer to the magic of history this is the ideal opportunity.

Make a present of the past

Step through the doors of a royal palace and you're surrounded by stories of strategy, intrigue, ambition, romance, devotion and disaster. What more inspiring gift could there be than a Historic Royal Palaces membership for someone who shares your love of history, amazing buildings, their beautiful contents and stunning gardens?

Contact us

If you would like to know more about how you can help Historic Royal Palaces, please contact the Development Department on 0203 166 6321 or email development@hrp.org.uk

To enquire about membership, either for yourself or as a gift, please call 0844 482 7788 or email members@hrp.org.uk

Volunteers wanted

Would you like to join the team at Historic Royal Palaces and help us with our work? Whether you could afford an afternoon each week or occasional hours we would value your support. In return, we can offer the special insights and intimacy with the palaces that working here can provide.

We believe that volunteers provide an important link between the historic buildings in our care, our visitors and the local community, and that volunteer support has a valuable role to play across all of the palaces within our care. The use of volunteers complements the work of our staff and enables us to further enrich and enhance the visitor experience and to undertake projects that we would not normally be able to carry out.

As an independent charity, we receive no funding from the Government or the Crown, so the support of visitors, members and volunteers is crucial.

In 2005, Historic Royal Palaces launched a volunteering programme to extend significantly the use of volunteers across the organisation. We would really like to encourage as many people as possible from the community to get actively involved in our work. Full training is given; many of our volunteers find that the skills they develop are useful in the wider job market.

Becoming a volunteer at Historic Royal Palaces means you will have the opportunity to participate at all levels and in a variety of different ways. These include roles such as room describers, information providers and family activity assistants.

For further information on volunteering opportunities within Historic Royal Palaces or to request a volunteer pack, please contact the Volunteer Manager on 0203 166 6183 or email volunteers@hrp.org.uk. Additional information about volunteering can be found on our website www.hrp.org.uk.

The private life of palaces

Hampton Court Palace Kew Palace Kensington Palace Banqueting House Tower of London

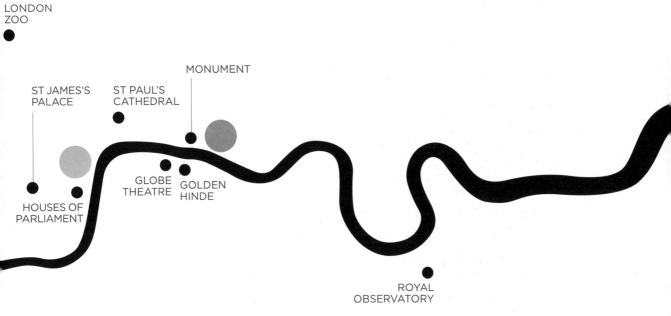

LONDON
ZOO

MONUMENT

ST JAMES'S
PALACE

ST PAUL'S
CATHEDRAL

GLOBE
THEATRE

GOLDEN
HINDE

HOUSES OF
PARLIAMENT

ROYAL
OBSERVATORY

1
Colonel Blood and the Crown Jewels

Early in the morning of 9 May 1671, Thomas Blood arrived at the Tower of London. He had been a visitor before, and was recognised by the guards. Leaving one man outside with the horses, Blood led three companions across to the Martin Tower: his son Thomas, Robert Perot and a man called Richard Halliwell who can best be described as a thug. All were secretly armed with knives, pocket pistols and swordsticks.

As they waited in the rooms belonging to Talbot Edwards, the Keeper of the Crown Jewels, Blood asked if his son could see the jewels. Edwards agreed and led his guests to the room downstairs. When they got there, Halliwell stood guard outside the door and the others quickly overpowered Edwards, tied him up and gagged him by ramming a piece of wood in his mouth. The old man was told that if he remained quiet he would come to no harm but he struggled so much that he was stabbed and given 'several unkind knocks on the head'. With Edwards immobilised, the three men helped themselves to the treasures in front of them. While Perot stuffed the orb down his breeches, Blood crushed the state crown and hid it under his cloak. He told his son to saw the sceptre in half and hide it in a bag.

So far their plan had worked brilliantly …

Thomas Blood's daring attempt to steal the Crown Jewels is perhaps one of the most mysterious episodes in the history of the Tower of London. It was the closest anybody has ever got to stealing the precious and sacred symbols of monarchy. Nobody knows exactly why Blood tried to steal them in the first place. And nobody knows why Charles II then not only pardoned him for doing so, but even granted him a pension.

Blood was an intriguing and complex character. He was a reckless, violent adventurer, yet he was also a deeply religious man, a nonconformist who claimed to avoid strong drink and loathed 'obscene and scurrilous talk'. His looks were striking. A contemporary described him as 'a tall rough-boned man, with small legs, a pock freckled face, with little hollow blue eyes'. Although he had seen some military service, his rank of 'Colonel' was purely of his own invention. Blood had prospered in Ireland after the Civil War but at the restoration of the monarchy in 1660 the new regime had confiscated some of his lands. This, together with his strong nonconformist religious sympathies, led him into a series of daring escapades. The first was in 1663 when he took an active part in an unsuccessful plot to seize Dublin Castle and overthrow the Duke of Ormonde, the Lord Lieutenant of Ireland, whom he blamed personally for his misfortune. Four years later Blood helped rescue his friend Captain John Mason, a fellow-plotter, who was being taken to York for trial and probable execution. In 1670 he ambushed his old enemy the Duke of Ormonde again, this time in London. Blood planned either to murder Ormonde, who he had never forgiven for the seizure of his lands and the execution of his friends following the failure in 1663, or to hold him to ransom. The scheme went badly wrong. Ormonde may have been elderly but he fought back vigorously and Blood and his accomplices were forced to flee.

Thomas Blood's '… pock freckled face, with little hollow blue eyes', but by all accounts this daring Crown Jewels thief was a charmer.

So it was that in 1671 Blood planned his most daring escapade yet, an attempt to steal the Crown Jewels. They were stored in the Martin Tower in the north-east corner of the Inner Ward. Talbot Edwards who looked after them was an elderly ex-soldier. He lived with his family in the rooms above and, for a small consideration, he would show visitors the jewels. In fact there was little of great antiquity on display. In 1649, having done away with the monarchy, the new republic duly did away with its regalia as well. The crowns were 'totally broken and defaced', the plate was sent to the Mint to be melted down into coinage and the remaining items were sold. As a result, at the Restoration all that could be found for the new king's coronation were the 17th-century ceremonial swords and the 12th-century coronation spoon. This was returned to the Tower by a Royalist sympathiser who had bought it at the sale in 1649. Everything else had to be remade in 1660, including the sovereign's orb and sceptre, the state crown and St Edward's coronation crown.

Blood and his fellow conspirators were imprisoned in the Tower, but the 'Colonel' somehow won a pardon and release from the King.

Exactly why Blood wanted to steal the Crown Jewels is not clear. His motives may just have been mercenary. Perhaps he carried out the raid as a slight on the monarchy, as part of a plan to gain access to the King to complain about his past treatment. Some say it was simply for the thrill of it. In any event, disguised as a clergyman, Blood began to make frequent visits to the Tower and soon befriended Edwards and his wife. So the day dawned when the plan was executed – and foiled.

Just as Blood and his accomplices prepared to make their way out of the Tower, fate intervened in the form of Talbot Edwards's son. Having been abroad for several years, he returned home unexpectedly that very morning and raised the alarm. The gang members tried to make their escape but, after a brief scuffle in which shots were fired, they were overpowered and captured. Blood remained remarkably unconcerned about his capture and when he was faced with interrogation in the Tower he demanded to see the King in person. Much to everyone's surprise, the King agreed and on 12 May the two men met in private.

What exactly passed between the King and Blood is not clear. It was later said that Blood admitted his part in the rescue of Mason and the attack on Ormonde and unleashed a torrent of blarney upon the wryly amused King. He even is said to have claimed that he had been involved in an earlier plot to kill Charles while he was bathing in the Thames but 'his heart misgave him out of awe of His Majesty'. When the King asked Blood what he would do if his life were spared, Blood is supposed to have replied that he would 'endeavour to deserve it'. On 18 July the Earl of Arlington, Charles's Secretary of State, arrived at the Tower bringing a warrant for Blood's release. Then, on 26 August, Blood received a full pardon for all his previous crimes and a grant of Irish lands worth £500 a year.

Why had the King pardoned Blood? Charles was clearly entertained by Blood's escapades. Perhaps they reminded him of his own experiences twenty years earlier when he too was involved in a series of hair-raising adventures while on the run from Oliver Cromwell's forces after defeat at the Battle of Worcester. He also clearly recognised Blood's value as a spy; over the next few years he used him as a source of information about the activities of the nonconformist community.

Or had Blood been working for the government as a double-agent all along? The papers of Joseph Williamson, the King's security chief, seem to suggest that. The truth may never be known.

The jewels were soon back on display, needless to say under conditions of much tighter security. The wooden bars guarding the regalia were replaced by iron ones and visitors were no longer allowed to handle the objects. Today they are kept under conditions of very high security in the Waterloo Barracks. The current display, which was opened by Her Majesty The Queen in 1994, attracts well over two million people every year. And more than three centuries after Blood's daring attempt to steal them, the security of the jewels still ultimately rests in the hands of an old soldier, the Resident Governor.

2
The most famous maze in the history of the world

'We'll just go in here, so that you can say you've been, but it's very simple.'

With those fateful words, Harris initiated the most famous of all visits to the world-celebrated Hampton Court Maze. The visit was a fictional one in Jerome K Jerome's comic novel *Three Men in a Boat* of 1889. 'It's absurd to call it a maze. You keep on taking the first turning to the right. We'll just walk around for ten minutes, and then go and get some lunch.'

As so often, fiction closely follows fact. For needless to say, Harris and his party got hopelessly lost. This did not prevent him from acting as an impromptu guide to a group of bemused tourists, many of whom 'had given up all hopes of either getting in or out, or of ever seeing their home and friends again'. Eventually, after several unsuccessful attempts to escape their unlikely prison, the party called for help, but the young keeper sent in to rescue them got lost himself. It was only when a more experienced keeper returned from his dinner that they were all set free at last.

It is most likely that it was William III who ordered the Maze's creation almost two centuries before Harris and his companions ventured in. Although Cardinal Wolsey was the first to build ornamental gardens at Hampton Court, it was Henry VIII who was responsible for establishing the structure of the palace gardens, with a privy

Left: A London Transport poster by Frederic Henri Kay Henrion promises a fun day out at Hampton Court for a school teacher and her charges in 1956.

Below: If this 1832 guide to the Maze was meant to help you get out, why is everyone stuck in the middle?

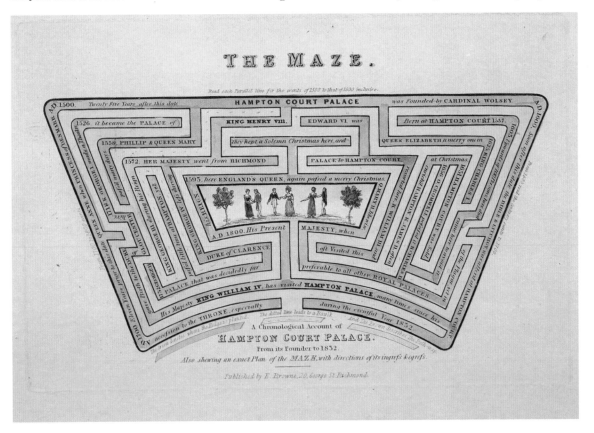

Left: William III's wilderness is glorious in the spring, the grass carpeted with over a million primroses, harebells, crocuses, narcissus and daffodils 'growing in wild profusion as nature intended'.

Right: These two early 20th-century visitors to Hampton Court were last seen turning left, or was it right? Today, around 330,000 people go in and, eventually, out of the Maze every year.

(or private) garden to the south, a public garden to the east, pleasure grounds and an orchard to the north and the entrance and tiltyard over to the west. This layout remained intact until the end of the 17th century and the reign of William and Mary. They decided to remodel the entire estate in the Baroque style, planting avenues of trees, creating a new privy garden to the south (stunningly restored following excavations in 1992-3), a great parterre to the east, a kitchen garden to the west and a wilderness to the north.

William clearly liked mazes, for he had previously created one at his Dutch home of Huis ten Bosch, the 'House in the Wood'. A drawing of Hampton Court made in 1702, the year William died, features the Wilderness and in it the Maze. The word 'wilderness' comes from the verb 'to wilder' meaning to lose one's way rather than any description of wildness. So a 17th-century wilderness was in fact quite a formal creation – a series of interconnecting paths lined with high clipped hedges through which a visitor could wander and get pleasurably lost. Parts of the Hampton Court Wilderness took this idea even further. Early 18th-century plans show that, in addition to its hornbeam hedges and elm trees, the area originally housed four separate mazes of varying shapes and sizes. All that remains today is the famous Hampton Court Maze. Shaped like a triangle with one point cut off, its whole area covers less than an acre but its winding paths are over half a mile long.

In 1724 Daniel Defoe gave the first description of the Maze in his *Tour Thro' the Whole Island of Great Britain*: 'The vacant ground, which was large, is very happily cast into a wilderness, with a labyrinth and espaliers … This labyrinth and wilderness is not only well designed and completely finished, but is perfectly well kept, and the espaliers filled exactly, at bottom to the very ground, and are led up to proportioned heights on the top; so that nothing of that kind can be more beautiful'. Within a generation tastes had changed. The 1742 edition of Defoe's *Tour* commented that the Wilderness was 'far from affording any Pleasure, since nothing can be more disagreeable than to be immured between Hedges'. A guidebook to the palace published in the very same year does not even mention the Maze at all.

Seen from above, the Maze looks astonishingly like the get-out-quick plan. This historic landmark – the oldest surviving hedge maze still in use – was once part of a much larger garden of paths and labyrinths that covered the entire area to the north of the palace.

A new sound installation has been created in the Maze to entice visitors along its winding corridors. The more people there are, the louder the sounds become. All is fairly peaceful just at the moment ...

The Maze soon regained its popularity, especially following Queen Victoria's decision in 1838 that the palace and its grounds 'should be thrown open to all her subjects without restriction'. According to an 1850 guidebook to Hampton Court, 'the great attraction here is the Maze or Labyrinth, which was formed in the early part of King William's reign. Many hours are spent by young persons, aye, and by the old too, in trying to discover the intricacies of the labyrinth. To the young, indeed, it is a great source of amusement and enjoyment'.

In 1856 control of the Maze was placed in the care of William Dobson who was charged with its maintenance in exchange for the right to collect from each visitor a fee 'not exceeding a penny per person'. Dobson was still in post in 1898 aged 74, collecting an estimated £200 a year, but he was eventually persuaded to retire and was replaced by a turnstile in 1900. Nearly 8,500 visitors passed through the turnstile in its first month of existence and by 1925 over 200,000 people were visiting the Maze every year.

Even by the time of Harris's visit the character of the Wilderness had changed considerably. Over the years the elms had grown huge while the hedges became thinner until the area lost its original formality. This process was hastened by the decision taken early in the 20th century to grass over many of the Wilderness paths and construct a rocky dell. Writing in 1935, Ernest Yates observed, 'The Wilderness today, except for the maze, has nothing formal about it. It is a modern "wild garden" and in spring one of the most beautiful spots anywhere near London, the fine trees just bursting into leaf, flowering shrubs in perfection, and the wide spaces of grass carpeted with primroses, harebells, crocuses, narcissus and daffodils growing in wild profusion as nature intended.' The elm trees are now gone, victims of Dutch Elm disease, but the spring daffodils remain a popular attraction. As does the Maze.

In many ways the Maze has been a victim of its own success which has led to considerable wear and tear and, unfortunately, occasional deliberate abuse. Although the Maze had originally been made entirely of hornbeam, the Victorians repaired it with a variety of other plants, including privet, yew and laurel. In the 1960s the Maze was replanted entirely in yew, which is much more robust than hornbeam and better able to cope with large numbers of visitors, yet is less authentic. The question of replanting in appropriate species is being actively assessed.

The Maze remains one of the best-known and most visited attractions at Hampton Court. A new display using audio and lighting effects with an art installation at the centre has recently been installed creating a sense of journey and arrival and – perhaps most important of all – interpreting it as a remarkable historic artefact. Visitors should not only understand it better but also value it more. The key message now to the hundreds of visitors who enter the Maze every day is, 'Enjoy it, but take care of it. It's a really rare survivor from history.' And people are still getting lost – come and see if you can get to the centre or if the attendant has to be called to your rescue.

3
'May you never die a Yeoman Warder'

Yeoman Warder Mark Anderson relaxes in the Tower of London Club after a long day on duty. The blue 'undress' uniform he wears was introduced in 1858 to replace the red and gold Tudor state dress, which is now worn by the Yeoman Warders only on ceremonial and state occasions.

On an evening in May, 2010, a group of uniformed men gathered on Tower Green. The occasion? The swearing in of the newest Yeoman Warder by Major General Keith Cima CB, Resident Governor of the Tower of London. After taking an oath of royal allegiance that dates back to 1337, Mark Anderson joined his new colleagues in the Yeoman Warders' Club for a toast, drunk in port and served from an 18th-century pewter bowl – a gift from a Yeoman Warder who was found to have been running a pub in Southwark when he should have been on duty!

Tradition requires the Chief Yeoman Warder to toast all new recruits with the words 'May you never die a Yeoman Warder'. The origins of this rather odd statement can be found in the fact that by the early 19th century the post of Yeoman Warder was being sold for 250 guineas. £250 would be returned to the Yeoman Warder on his retirement with the balance kept by the Constable who appointed him but if the Yeoman Warder died in post, the Constable inherited the whole amount! However, the Duke of Wellington, who became Constable in 1826, was determined that the post of Yeoman Warder should be a reward for meritorious military service. He abolished this purchase system and decreed that from then on the post should be occupied by worthy army non-commissioned officers (NCOs).

The Duke's wishes are still adhered to today. To qualify as a 'Yeoman Warder of Her Majesty's Royal Palace and Fortress the Tower of London, and Member of the Sovereign's Body Guard of the Yeoman Guard Extraordinary', to give the post its proper title, you must have been a senior NCO in one of the Armed Services and hold a Military Long Service and Good Conduct Medal. Mark Anderson joined the Body of Yeoman Warders after 33 years Army service in the Royal Corps of Signals. During his career he was a member of the 'White Helmets', where he was part of the Corp's motorcycle display team! Mark's also seen active service in the first Gulf War, in Bosnia and Northern Ireland, where he was part of a bomb disposal unit. He also spent two years in working in Oman as an advisor to the Sultan's forces. May he never die a Yeoman Warder!

4
'As mechanical as the clock'

Above: George II's only major architectural work at Hampton Court was a suite of lodgings built in 1732 for his second son, William Augustus, Duke of Cumberland. The Prime Minister, Sir Robert Walpole, insisted that the new work should be designed to match the Tudor brickwork around it.

Left: *The Music Party* by Philippe Mercier, 1733. Frederick, Prince of Wales and his sisters appear to enjoy a moment of family harmony. In reality, the Prince was on bad terms with his sisters – but was passionately devoted to the cello.

The accession of George II in June 1727 brought to an end what had been ten years of near-abandonment for Hampton Court Palace and ushered in a decade of regular use, for the palace was George's favourite summer residence. Many of the interiors were refurbished under George and new accommodation was created for his second son, the Duke of Cumberland. Queen Caroline may have been the leading light as it is uncertain how involved the King was himself in this work as he claimed to hate the arts. 'I hate all boets and bainters' he is said to have once growled. George's great love was the army. He never tired of reminiscing of his experiences as a cavalry commander during the War of the Spanish Succession, and he was the last English monarch to command an army in battle, at Dettingen in 1743.

George and his wife Caroline of Ansbach established a strictly regimented pattern for court life at the palace. The full range of aristocratic and elite society was represented there, and courtiers followed a set routine. Particular days were set aside for specific activities. In 1731, the Countess of Pomfrett observed that 'all our actions are as mechanical as the clock which directs them' and Lord John Hervey, Vice-Chamberlain at court, later wrote:

> No mill-horse ever went in a more constant track, or more unchanging circle, so that by the assistance of an almanac for the day of the week, and a watch for the hour of the day, you may inform yourself fully, without any other intelligence but your memory, of every transaction within the verge of the court. Walking, chaises, levées and audiences fill the morning; at night the king plays at commerce and backgammon, and the queen at quadrille.

Even George's love life was governed by the clock. He would often be seen in the evening pacing up and down outside the apartments of Henrietta Howard, his mistress at the time, looking at his pocket watch and waiting for seven o'clock when he would go in and spend three hours or so with her before returning to his wife. George's relationship with Henrietta Howard is often described as an oddly passionless one, and that he took a mistress because it was expected of him as a king rather than from any particular desire. Having said that, there is the fact that he hated reading and she was deaf …

In addition to the occasional diplomatic reception, three of the most important public activities carried out at court were the morning levée (when the King rose from his bed), dining in public and the evening drawing room. During his levée the King spoke to his ministers, guests and members of his family, using the occasion as an opportunity to make his thoughts public. Not even illness would prevent the King from staging his levée. According to Hervey, George would 'get out of bed in a high fever, only to dress and have a levée, and in five minutes undress and return to bed until the same ridiculous farce of health the next day at the same hour'.

Unlike his father, George always recognised the importance of being seen by his subjects, and on Thursdays and Sundays he and his family would dine in public. He had even done this as Prince of

Wales, when at times he ran a rival court to that of his father.

In 1717 the Bishop of Lichfield noted that 'he dines openly and with company every day and the novelty of the sight draws a mighty concourse'. In 1733 a visitor to Hampton Court wrote that the King's 'table is placed in the midst of a hall, surrounded by benches to the very ceiling, which are filled with an infinite number of spectators'. On one occasion the crush was so great that 'the rail surrounding the table broke and causing some to fall, made a diverting scramble for hats and wigs at which their majesties laughed heartily'. The King's Eating Room turned out to be too small to accommodate the hordes of royal-watchers and so most public dining took place in the Queen's State Apartments in the much larger Music Room, now called the Public Dining Room.

Public drawing rooms normally started at ten o'clock when the royal family would enter the Queen's Drawing Room, which had been set up with tables and chairs, and then circulate for an hour or so before retiring.

It had been a tradition since the 15th century that if the king and queen wished to sleep together they would do so in the queen's private bedchamber as even the king's private rooms were full of courtiers. The queen's rooms were much quieter and her Ladies of the Bedchamber were much less intrusive. Thus George and Caroline slept together in the bedchamber in the Queen's Private Apartments at Hampton Court. In 1995 these rooms were restored to the way they would have looked in the 1730s. The original bed has not survived but the special locks on the door that enabled the King and Queen to lock themselves in at night using cords which ran to their bedside can still be seen. Among Queen Caroline's Ladies of the Bedchamber was her husband's mistress, Henrietta Howard, and the Queen took special delight in ensuring she was given the most menial tasks to perform.

Wednesdays and Saturdays were set aside for stag hunting, which George II loved and considered more fitting for the dignity of a king than chasing after a fox. He particularly enjoyed hunting in Richmond Park where he would be followed by so many courtiers and servants that in the end tickets had to be sold to those wishing to join in the fun. The Queen, who was not a good horsewoman, followed in a four-wheeled chaise, normally gossiping with Lord Hervey. George was a very energetic huntsman and would sometimes chase a stag up to 40 miles. His mistress Henrietta Howard once wrote 'we hunt with great noise and violence, and have every day a tolerable chance to have a neck broke'. Between November 1731 and January 1734, the royal hunting party accounted for 100 stags and 64 hinds.

Relations between the King and Queen and their son Frederick, Prince of Wales were no better than George's had been with his own father and the court's last visit to Hampton Court, in 1737, was overshadowed by an almighty row over the pregnancy of Frederick's wife, Augusta, Princess of Wales. The Queen was determined that the Princess's confinement should be at Hampton Court where she could supervise the birth. Thus she would ensure that Frederick, whom she considered incapable of fathering a healthy child, did not secretly introduce a substitute for a sickly royal baby. Frederick was equally determined that the birth should be in London and when, on 31 July, the Princess went into premature labour he had her whisked off to St James's Palace before his parents knew anything about it. When a servant woke Caroline and told her what had happened the Queen hurried up to London but arrived too late to witness the birth of a baby girl who died soon afterwards. The incident caused the final breakdown in relations between the King and the Prince of Wales and on 10 September George sent Frederick a letter ordering him to leave St James's Palace.

That November the Queen died from complications arising from her own last pregnancy. Although George lived for another 23 years he never brought his court back to Hampton Court Palace again. With those events almost three centuries ago, royal residence at the palace ceased.

Above: The Queen's Private Bedchamber – which unlike the King's was free from intrusive courtiers – provided a retreat for the royal couple.

Left: An 18th-century court scene showing 'The ceremony of introducing a Lady to Her Majesty'. At this time, it was compulsory for ladies at court to wear hoops under their dresses. One exhausted lady remarked, 'I stood from two to four in the Drawing Room and of course loaded with a great hoop of no inconsiderable weight.'

Previous: The strolling hour: a tiring afternoon's work at court in the 1730s. Daily life followed a strict routine, which irritated many who were obliged to conform to their Majesties' pleasure: 'No mill-horse ever went in a more constant track, or more unchanging circle' yawned the Vice-Chamberlain, John Hervey.

THE

KING'

NAGEI

ROYAL,

TOWEI

LONDO

THIS ANCIENT EDIFICE,

Reign of Edward IV. in the

FOR THE RECEPTION OF

gn Beast, Bird

5
The first London zoo

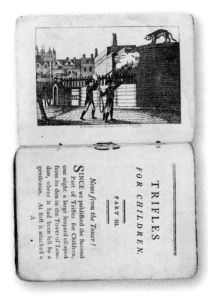

Above: News from the Tower! There was a leopard on the loose at the fortress, according to this late 18th-century children's booklet. Although 'greatly delighted with its acquired liberty', the animal was later shot by a soldier.

Left: The Tower Menagerie was a powerful attraction in 1826. The formidable array of animals included a pair of 'handsome hunting leopards', 'an enormous grisly bear', 'a crocodile from the River Nile' and two kangaroos.

In 1830 and then again in 1835, wagons with specially reinforced and barred cages trundled away from the Tower of London, carrying off wild beasts. The first consignment – 150 animals with a pair of rather bedraggled lions, a panther, leopard, tiger and bear at their head – was heading for Regent's Park. They would form a nucleus of the new London Zoo. The second and larger group were shipped much further, to the USA. On the orders of the Duke of Wellington and exactly 600 years after it was founded, the Tower Menagerie was no more. Now it is largely forgotten. Yet the visitors who warily approach the Tower ravens are following in the footsteps of many generations of visitors who came to marvel not just at birds but at much more dangerous creatures.

King John seems to have been the first monarch to keep a royal lion in the Tower, soon after 1200. The key moment in the history of the Menagerie came in 1235 when the Holy Roman Emperor, Frederick II gave three leopards to Henry III, doubtless in honour of Henry's coat of arms. In 1251 the leopards were joined by a 'white bear', generally assumed to be a polar bear. He was a present from the King of Norway, and the Sheriffs of London were ordered to pay for his maintenance and to provide a muzzle, an iron chain and a rope long enough to allow him to hunt for fish in the Thames. In 1255 Henry's collection received its most exciting addition yet when Louis IX of France presented him with an African elephant (the first to be seen in Britain since the Roman invasion of AD 43). The elephant caused a sensation and amongst the many that flocked to marvel at it was the historian Matthew Paris who took the opportunity to draw the great beast from life.

The Menagerie continued to flourish throughout the Middle Ages. From the 1330s the animals were housed in the now-vanished Lion Tower at the south-western approach to the Byward Tower (the main landward gateway). This was to be the Menagerie's home for the next 500 years. By the 16th century the Menagerie had developed into a major tourist attraction. In 1598 Paul Hentzner, a German visitor to London, recorded that:

> On coming out of the Tower we were led to a small house, close by, where are kept a variety of creatures … three lionesses, one lion of great size, called Edward IV from his having been born in that reign; a tiger; a lynx; a wolf excessively old … a porcupine and an eagle. All these creatures are kept in a place, fitted up for the purpose with wooden lattices at the Queen's expense.

Whoever gave Hentzner his information must have been encouraging exaggeration, for if Edward IV the lion had really been born in the reign of his regal namesake, he would have been at least 115 years old.

At the start of the 17th century, James I took a great interest in his collection of beasts. During his reign the Menagerie was enlarged and its facilities refurbished. The upper levels of the two-storey lion cages were fitted with channels to carry away the creatures' urine

and stairs were installed to allow the animals to climb from one level to another. An exercise yard was created in part of the moat around the Lion Tower, and within the yard itself the King's masons built 'a great cistern … for the lions to drink and wash themselves in'. These improvements seem to suggest an almost modern concern for the welfare of the animals – yet the exercise yard was also used to 'bait the lions with dogs, bears, bulls, boars etc' for the amusement of the King. A large viewing platform was erected just to enable him to watch the fun. On one occasion James was bitterly disappointed when a bear which had killed a child was pitted against one of the Tower's lions, only for the two creatures to refuse to fight. Feeding time was a particularly popular occasion as it offered the spectacle of living creatures, including dogs and cats brought by the visitors themselves, being given to the animals to kill and eat.

By modern standards the arrangements made for the safety of visitors left much to be desired. The female leopard which, late in the Menagerie's history, 'evinced a particular predilection for the destruction of umbrellas, parasols, muffs, hats, and other such articles of dress as may happen to come within her reach' may have caused amusement but there were also tragic incidents. In 1686 the daughter of one of the keepers was mauled by a lion. According to a contemporary pamphlet, it was a bloody sight:

A mid-18th-century guidebook warned visitors to be wary of a large baboon that was very skilful at throwing objects including stools, bowls or anything else within his reach.

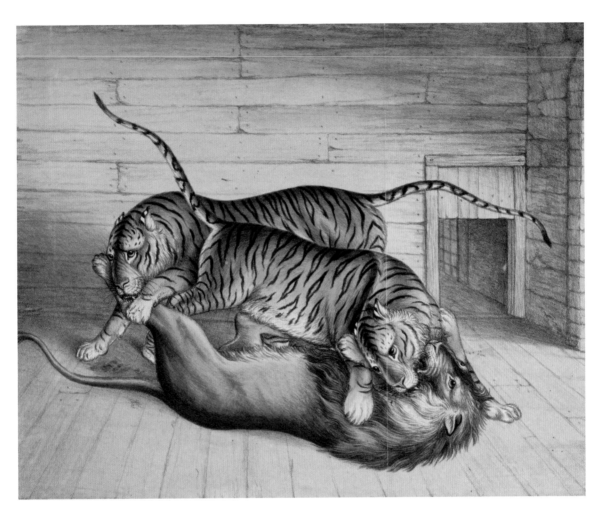

Top: The 'extraordinary and fatal combat' between the lion, tiger and tigress that took place in the Tower Menagerie in December 1830. 'The roaring and yelling of the combatants resounded through the yards, and excited in the various animals the most lively demonstrations of fear or rage'.

Bottom: An invitation to view the annual ceremony of washing the lions – on April Fools' Day 1857.

one of the lions (being the greatest there) putting out his paw, she was so venturous as to stroke him as she used to do, but suddenly [he] caught her by the middle of the arm with his claws and mouth, and most miserably tore her flesh from the bone, before he could be unloosed, notwithstanding they thrust several lighted torches at him, but at last they got her away, whereupon surgeons were immediately sent for, who after some time thought it necessary for the preservation of her life, to cut off her arm, but she died not many hours after …

By the end of the 18th century the school of monkeys was one of the Menagerie's principal attractions, but the fact that visitors were allowed to enter the 'schoolroom' without a barrier between them and the monkeys probably contributed to an incident which led to its closure. An 1810 guidebook noted that 'formerly several monkeys were kept, but one of them having torn a boy's leg in a dangerous manner they were removed'. It was not only the visitors who suffered from lax security. In December 1830 a keeper accidentally allowed a lion, a tiger and a tigress into the same cage; the lion was so badly injured in the ensuing fight that he died within a few days. This was not the first time that one of the animals came to an untimely end. In 1791 a Tower ostrich died – it was said – after making a feast of

NERO, a Lion from SENEGAL.

The Elephant presented to their Majesties, 27th Sept. 1763.

Above: 'The elephant presented to their Majesties', 27 September 1763. The first elephant to join the royal menagerie arrived at the Tower in 1255.

Left: One of the main attractions: Nero, a lion from Senegal. So successful was the breeding of lions at the Tower in the late 18th century that one guidebook proclaimed, 'we may boast now of an uninterrupted line of *British* lions'.

80 nails; and in 1828 a keeper wrote that 'the Secretary bird, having incautiously introduced its long neck into the den of the hyena, was deprived of it and its head at one bite'.

The Menagerie had continued to flourish through the 17th and 18th centuries, and in 1741 the first true guidebook to the Tower listed the animals on display and recorded their often disappointingly everyday names. The collection included Marco and Phillis the lions and their son Nero, another two lionesses called Jenny and Nanny, a leopard called Will, a panther called Jenny, two tigers confusingly also called Will and Phillis with their son Dick, as well as a racoon, two vultures, two eagles, an ape and a porcupine whose names went unrecorded. However, by the early 19th century, the fortunes of the Menagerie were in decline and by 1821 all that remained were four lions, a panther, a leopard, a grizzly bear and a tiger.

The Menagerie enjoyed a brief revival when Alfred Cops was appointed keeper in 1822 for he added animals he had purchased himself and soon amassed a collection of 60 species and 280 animals. The recovery was short-lived and in 1830 the decision was taken to transfer the royal collection of beasts to the newly-established Zoological Society of London in Regent's Park. Cops continued to display his own collections in the Tower for a few more years but in 1835, under pressure from the now exasperated authorities, he sold his animals to an American showman who shipped them across the Atlantic.

Soon the Lion Tower itself would be dismantled. Two recently-excavated lions' skulls from the 14th century are all that remain of the Tower's most unusual visitor attraction.

6
A taste of palace history

Left: A rather precarious way to harvest the Great Vine in August 1960.

Above: Vine Keeper Gillian Strudwick is doing the same job today, minus the stilettos! Always a magnet for sightseers, the vine became a literal 'tourist trap' at the end of the 19th century. On bank holidays over 10,000 people squeezed in, and out, of a narrow doorway for a peek at the famous plant. The viewing part of the Vine House was rebuilt in 1902 with a new entry and exit system which improved the visitor experience considerably.

In 1768 the Surveyor to His Majesty's Gardens and Waters at Hampton Court Palace, Lancelot 'Capability' Brown, planted a cutting from a vine at Valentines Park (Essex) in the palace gardens. Carefully tended over the years and protected by a succession of glasshouses, that small cutting has grown into the oldest and largest known vine in the world – the Great Vine at Hampton Court. Gillian Cox, the palace's full-time Vine Keeper, cares for this historic plant, which measures over 3.6 metres (12 feet) around the base and has rods up to 36 metres (120 feet) in length. She spends most of her working time in the current glasshouse. Although this was built in 1969, it still retains its wrought iron Victorian supports and the wooden 19th-century frame that holds up the vine.

The vine itself is a common variety – a Black Hamburg – which produces succulent bunches of sweet black dessert grapes. Gillian's duties include pruning the vine in winter, nipping out shoots to keep its growth under control and managing its crop by thinning out the bunches. The vine still produces 227-318kg (500-700lbs) of grapes each year and inevitably the Vine Keeper's busiest time comes at the end of August when the grapes are ready to be harvested. It usually takes about three weeks to pick and package them all and Gillian is helped in this task by a team of volunteers. The grapes were originally produced for consumption by the royal household but in 1930 George V started sending them to hospitals and within five years they were being sold to palace visitors. This is still the case today, with bunches being delivered to the palace shops on a daily basis in late August and early September. So visit the palace at that time of year and you'll have a wonderful opportunity to get a real taste of palace history by buying and eating grapes from the most famous vine in the world.

Gillian Strudwick, Vine Keeper

7
A poignant place of execution

Above: The Banqueting House, through which Charles I walked to the scaffold.

Left: Charles I by Sir Anthony van Dyck (detail), c1635. On 27 January 1649, the King was found guilty of treason. His death warrant stated that he 'be put to death by the severing of his head from his body'.

It was the morning of 11 November 1647 and Charles I was in residence at Hampton Court Palace. When the King did not emerge from his apartments at the normal time, his attendants told Colonel Edward Whalley who was waiting to see him that Charles was still writing letters in his bedchamber. Whalley later wrote, 'I waited there without mistrust till six of the clock; then I began to doubt, and told the bedchamber-men, Mr Maule and Mr Murray, I wondered the king was so long a-writing.' Although a hard-bitten man, even Whalley baulked at disturbing a king and he was reduced to peering through the royal keyhole in a vain attempt to see what was happening. Finally Whalley's patience snapped. He demanded to be let into the King's apartments via the Privy Stairs at the back, only to find that the rooms were empty. The King had gone. To use his own phrase, the bird had flown.

Charles I had not been staying in his palace in the usual way, but was a captive. Whalley was his guard. The King had escaped across the garden and crossed the Thames by boat, accompanied by a small band of supporters.

Eighteen months before, in May 1646, Charles had been facing defeat in the English Civil War. He had surrendered to the Scottish army in the hope of winning their support for his cause. Negotiations failed and the Scots handed him over to his sworn enemy, the English Parliament. The Parliamentary forces kept the King under loose house arrest at Holdenby House in the Midlands. There were many in the victorious 'Roundhead' Army who were concerned that they might be excluded from any agreement that Charles made with Parliament and so, on 4 June 1647, a force of soldiers under Cornet George Joyce seized the King, probably with the connivance of Oliver Cromwell. Even at this late stage, very few Parliamentarians could envisage a settlement that did not include Charles as King, so Charles was not imprisoned in the Tower of London but was installed in Hampton Court Palace instead. There he lived more 'as a guarded and attended prince than as a conquered and purchased captive'.

In command of Charles's guard at Hampton Court was Colonel Edward Whalley. He was a cousin of Oliver Cromwell and a veteran of the great battles of Marston Moor and Naseby. Whalley seems to have treated the King with courtesy and fairness and when Charles fled he even left behind a letter thanking Whalley for his kindness. During his time there Charles was permitted to see his children and was visited by representatives of both Parliament and the Army, neither of which had given up hope of reaching some form of compromise.

At exactly the time that Charles was being held at Hampton Court Palace, downstream at Putney representatives from the victorious Parliamentary Army were debating the very basis of political society. There Colonel Rainsborough uttered the radical sentiment, 'I think the poorest he in England has a life to lead as the greatest he'. The franchise, controls on elected authority and stringent curbs on the power of monarchy were among the topics debated. There were those who envisaged an end to the rule of kings. The 'greatest he' would be cut down to size. The call to liberty was a rousing one and the memory of the Putney Debates became a touchstone for radicalism.

Liberty for Charles himself did not last long. Having escaped from Hampton Court, the King took refuge with the Earl of Southampton before fleeing to the Isle of Wight where he hoped that the island's governor, Colonel Robert Hammond, would help him. The King and his companions had misjudged Hammond, who refused to betray the Parliamentarian cause. Charles found himself a prisoner once more, this time in Carisbrooke Castle. Even now he continued to meet representatives of Parliament, the Army and the Scots but he could not cease plotting. His involvement in the Royalist risings and the Scottish invasion in the summer of 1648 finally convinced many leaders of the Army, including Oliver Cromwell, that the King had to be destroyed.

Charles was taken from Carisbrooke to the grim fortress of Hurst Castle, perched on a shingle spit in the Solent, and then to Windsor Castle to await his trial before a specially-convened High Court of Justice sitting in Westminster Hall. On 27 January 1649 Charles was found guilty of having 'traitorously and maliciously levied war against the present parliament and the people therein represented' and was sentenced to death. Among those who signed his death warrant was Edward Whalley.

The date for Charles's execution was set for 30 January 1649, the place was to be Whitehall Palace and the executioner's axe was brought in readiness from the Tower of London. The usual waist-high execution block could not be found and a much lower one, normally used for dismembering traitors, had to be sent in its place.

On the morning that he was to die Charles was held at St James's Palace where his two youngest children, Princess Elizabeth and Henry, Duke of Gloucester, were brought to him to say their tearful farewells. At ten o'clock, guarded by halberdiers, the King set out across St James's Park and entered Whitehall Palace for the last time. He was taken to his private apartments in the company of William Juxon, the Bishop of London, and spent the morning calmly at prayer.

Above left: *The King's Escape from Hampton Court.* The ease with which Charles escaped from the palace has raised the suggestion that he was encouraged or facilitated by his captors.

Above: *The Execution of Charles I* on 30 January 1649, by an unknown artist. At the King's signal that he was ready, the executioner severed his head with one blow. A great groan went up from the crowd who had gathered to watch.

Although the King had intended to eat nothing, Juxon persuaded him to take bread and wine to keep his strength up and as a final Communion. Charles also put on an extra shirt for fear that he might shiver in the bitter cold and cause his enemies to think that he was afraid. Eventually the King was led out through the galleries of the palace and into the Banqueting House, beneath the painted ceiling that glorified the name of Stuart and his father James I. From here Charles went out from the landing of the staircase, through where a window had been, on to a wooden scaffold. According to one observer the King stepped out on to the scaffold as calmly as if going to one of the court masques that the Banqueting House had once hosted.

Refused permission to address the crowd, Charles spoke to those around him on the scaffold. In his final speech he sought to justify his actions. He finished by declaring that he was going 'from a corruptible to an incorruptible crown, where no disturbance can be'. Taking off his cloak and the badge of the Order of the Garter and giving them to Bishop Juxon, Charles laid his head upon the block and stretched out his hands to indicate that he was ready. The executioner severed his head with one blow. According to an onlooker, as the axe fell 'there was such a dismal universal groan amongst the thousands of people

Above: The Banqueting House is all that remains of Whitehall Palace. Many plans were produced for rebuilding the palace after the fire in 1698, but they remained on the drawing board.

Left: Detail of the Banqueting House ceiling, Peter Paul Rubens's baroque masterpiece, showing *The Peaceful Reign of James I, or the Benefits of his Government.*

who were in sight of it, as it were with one consent, as I have never heard before and desire I may not hear again'.

Concerned that Charles's grave might become a place of pilgrimage, the new regime had his corpse sent by water to Windsor and the decapitated monarch was buried within the castle walls in St George's Chapel.

The Banqueting House is the only remaining complete building of Whitehall Palace, the sovereign's principal residence from 1530 until 1698 (when it was destroyed by fire). Designed by Inigo Jones for James I, the classical Banqueting House was originally built for masques, plays and state occasions and is still used today for royal, government and society events. It seems ironic that it will always be best remembered not for these ceremonies and revels but for a far grimmer performance – the execution of a king.

8
'I will be good'

Above: A 'rather melancholy childhood'; Princess Victoria's self-portrait, 1832, aged 13.

Left: Queen Victoria by Franz Xaver Winterhalter, 1855. Although her childhood at Kensington had often been lonely, Victoria later wrote, 'Still I am fond of the poor old Palace'.

In 1818, Edward, Duke of Kent married Victoria, Dowager Princess of Leiningen in a joint ceremony at Kew Palace with his elder brother the Duke of Clarence, the future William IV, who gave up his long-standing mistress and the mother of his many children to marry Princess Adelaide of Saxe-Meiningen. Heavily in debt, Edward was forced to live overseas with his new wife but when she became pregnant they returned to England to live in Kensington Palace and await events.

On 24 May 1819 the Duchess gave birth to a daughter, according to tradition in the North Drawing Room of the Kents' apartments in the palace. The following month the young Princess was christened in a private ceremony in the Cupola Room. The Prince Regent, whose daughter and heir, Charlotte, had recently died, refused to allow either Charlotte or Augusta to be included in the child's names but did support the Duke's suggestion of Alexandrina, after her godfather Alexander I, Tsar of Russia. He then suggested that her second name should be that of her mother – Victoria. Less than nine months later the Duke died unexpectedly and the Duchess and her baby daughter left the rented house in Sidmouth in which they had been staying for reasons of economy and returned to Kensington Palace.

They were now literally penniless, the Duke's furniture had been taken by his creditors and it was only thanks to the generosity of her brother Leopold that the Duchess was able to refurnish their apartments. At the age of five the young Princess was taken into the care of Louise Lehzen, governess to Princess Feodora, the Duchess's daughter by her first marriage. Victoria's education was placed in the hands of professional tutors but Lehzen taught her history. It was during one of these lessons that Victoria was given a genealogy of the royal houses of Europe to study and realisation dawned. She saw that one day she would be queen and famously declared, 'I will be good'.

Princess Victoria led a somewhat isolated life at Kensington but enjoyed the company of her elder half-sister until Feodora married in 1828. Louise Lehzen also played with the young Princess, helping her to dress her collection of 132 dolls, and she remained a close confidante until Victoria's own marriage in 1840. Victoria was also allowed considerable freedom to be driven and later to drive herself around Kensington Gardens in a pony carriage. Her happiest times, however, seem to have been spent at her Uncle Leopold's house at Claremont in Surrey, which she later described as 'the brightest epoch of my otherwise rather melancholy childhood'. Victoria was to have a less than happy relationship with Sir John Conroy, a former friend of her father's who was now her mother's chamberlain and confidant. In order to maintain what he believed was Victoria's dependence on her mother, and thus on him, he instituted 'regulations' to prevent her from meeting new people. Victoria despised him and had her revenge at her accession when she refused all his demands for a pension, a peerage and a position at court. One person she did manage to meet, however, was her cousin Prince Albert of Saxe-Coburg, whose visit was arranged by her mother with a view to a potential marriage.

Above: *The First Council of Queen Victoria* by Sir David Wilkie, 1838. To make the young Queen stand out, Wilkie painted Victoria in a white dress. In reality she wore mourning black.

Right: Queen Victoria's accession dress, the colour faded, survives in the collection at Kensington Palace.

Victoria was immediately taken with Albert, writing in her diary that he was 'extremely handsome … full of goodness and sweetness and very clever and intelligent'.

In August 1836 William IV visited Kensington Palace and found to his fury that the Duchess of Kent had taken over a number of the state rooms on the second floor and adapted them for her own use. William complained publicly that 'a most unwarrantable liberty had been taken with one of his Palaces' and that this had been done 'not only without his consent, but contrary to his commands'. Still angry the following day, which was his birthday, he made a speech in which he expressed the hope that he would live long enough for Victoria to succeed him as queen in her own right and not be placed under a regency led by her mother. The King's wish came true. On 24 May 1837 the Princess celebrated her 18th birthday and four weeks later William died at Windsor in the early hours of the morning of 20 June. The Archbishop of Canterbury, William Howley, and the Lord Chamberlain, Lord Conyngham, rode straight to Kensington to break the news to Victoria. She later wrote:

> I was awoke at 6 o'clock by Mamma who told me that the archbishop of Canterbury and Lord Conyngham were here and wished to see me. I got out of bed and went into my sitting room (only in my dressing gown) and <u>alone</u>, and saw them. Lord Conyngham then acquainted me that my poor Uncle, the King, was no more … and consequently that <u>I</u> am <u>Queen</u>.

Three hours later she received the Prime Minister, Lord Melbourne, and informed him that she wished him to remain in office. At eleven o'clock she held her first Privy Council meeting in what is now called the Red Saloon at Kensington Palace. Charles

Left: A conservator prepares one of Her Majesty Queen Elizabeth II's evening dresses for display at Kensington Palace.

Right: William III was Kensington's first royal owner and his statue stands in the grounds of the palace that he built. It was presented to Edward VII by his nephew, Kaiser Wilhelm II in 1907.

Greville, Clerk to the Privy Council, wrote in his diary that 'her extreme youth and inexperience, and the ignorance of the world concerning her, naturally excited intense curiosity'. However, all those present were extremely impressed by her performance. Greville continued, 'She bowed to the Lords, took her seat, and then read her speech in a clear, distinct and audible voice, and without any outward appearance of fear or embarrassment … going through the whole ceremony … with perfect calmness and self possession, but at the same time with a graceful modesty and propriety particularly interesting and ingratiating'. The Duke of Wellington, the victor at Waterloo more than twenty years before, who was also present, wrote that 'she was as gracious in her manner as if she had been performing the part for years'.

This scene was recorded in a painting of 1838 by Sir David Wilkie. To make the young Queen stand out Wilkie depicted her wearing a white dress, but as she was in mourning for the dead King she actually wore a black one. The dress still survives, along with her coronation robes, in the Royal Ceremonial Dress Collection, which is housed in Kensington Palace. Originally established as the Court Dress Collection, it was opened to the public by Princess Margaret on 24 May 1984, the 165th anniversary of Queen Victoria's birth.

The permanent displays tell the story of the design, manufacture and wearing of court dress. Royal dress is an important feature of the collection and the displays include dresses on loan from Her Majesty The Queen and dresses that belonged to the late Diana, Princess of Wales. For conservation reasons the items on display are changed regularly, which means that anyone making a return visit to the collection is always likely to find something new to enjoy. The 2002-3 exhibition *A Century of Queens' Wedding Dresses* included the stunning bridal outfit of Her Majesty The Queen which she wore in 1947, her mother's wedding dress, and the dress in which Queen Victoria was married to Prince Albert. Victoria may have moved to Buckingham Palace at her accession in 1837, but her presence at Kensington Palace is still keenly felt.

9
'The finest and most artistic in England'

Details from *Eliezer and Rebekah at the Well*. The *Abraham* tapestries appear in Henry VIII's inventory of 1548 as 'Tenne peces of newe arras of thistorie of Abraham'. They were valued at £10 a yard, or £8,260, at the time of the Commonwealth.

It is recorded in the Old Testament book of *Genesis* that Ishmael, son of Abraham, was cursed. 'His hand will be against every man, and every man's hand will be against him.' Ishmael, Abraham's first-born son by the maidservant Hagar, was to be rejected in favour of Isaac, his second son, born to his wife Sarah. From Isaac the Jewish people, the chosen people of God, were to flow.

Every picture tells a story, and at Hampton Court Palace every tapestry tells a story too. Abraham's rejection of Hagar and Ishmael is told in the sixth of a great series of woven tapestries that hang today in the setting for which they were commissioned, the Great Hall of Henry VIII's palace. The particular story that this scene represents has a meaning that would once have been obvious to anyone who saw it in all its shining glory. Henry VIII had finally secured the future of his dynasty with the birth of a son, Edward. The Prince's half-sisters Mary and Elizabeth were to be rejected by their father. From Edward a new future would undoubtedly flow.

With the benefit of hindsight we know that these hopes would be dashed: Edward would become king but he died young, and both his half-sisters succeeded him in turn bringing with them a maelstrom of religious division and strife. Henry's direct line had failed by 1603. Only the hopes expressed in a series of sumptuous wall hangings survive.

The earliest surviving works on display at Hampton Court Palace are those collected by Cardinal Wolsey and Henry VIII and the remains of this collection of tapestry are of international importance. In the 16th century tapestry was the most valued form of art, far more highly-prized than easel painting, and Henry spent lavishly on his collection which numbered more than 2,000 pieces. The *History of Abraham*, displayed on the walls of the Great Hall, is the most important set of all and the finest 16th-century set of tapestries in Britain today.

Measuring 81 metres (265 feet) in length and nearly 5 metres (16 feet) high, the full set consists of ten scenes showing the main events of Abraham's life. Each of the scenes is surrounded by a wide decorative border filled with allegorical and symbolic figures personifying the virtues and vices of the characters inside. They have faded now, the colours have degraded and the silver has tarnished, but their power and majesty survives. Tapestries like the *Abraham* series were much more than just a sumptuous and extremely expensive way of covering wall space – they were also subtle propaganda. Parallels could be drawn between their subject matter and the lives and aspirations of their owners. The *Abraham* tapestries sought to compare Henry, the new Head of the English Church and in effect patriarch to his people, with Abraham. The story of Abraham and Isaac had a particular appeal to Henry following the birth in 1537 of Edward, his long-awaited son and heir. Several of the individual scenes in the tapestries reinforced the dynastic message. The fourth scene shows the high priest Melchizedek blessing and supporting Abraham – exactly the kind of reaction that Henry was looking for from the senior clergy of the English Church.

The tapestries were woven in the Brussels workshop of Willem de Kempeneer. They were probably commissioned by Henry around 1540 or 1541 and delivered to England by 1543. Similar tapestries of the *Abraham* design exist in Vienna, Madrid and Toledo, but the Hampton Court version is by far the most sumptuous. Whereas the other versions are woven in wool and silk alone, Henry's set includes substantial amounts of gold and silver thread. The cost of the *Abraham* tapestries has been estimated at £2,000, a phenomenal sum at a time when a court painter like Holbein was receiving a salary of £30 a year. It is often said that each tapestry cost the equivalent of a warship. Late 16th and early 17th-century visitors frequently commented on their magnificence. At the sale of the royal art collection in 1651, during the Commonwealth, the *Abraham* tapestries were valued at £8,260, making them the most valuable work of art after the Crown Jewels. In the event the set was retained by Oliver Cromwell following his appointment as Lord Protector, and this ensured that they remained at Hampton Court Palace until the Restoration.

Although it seems that the *Abraham* tapestries were purchased for use in the Great Hall at Hampton Court, they were only hung there on special occasions and less valuable pieces took their place at other times. Indeed, when the agent of Cardinal Mazarin of France was trying to purchase the tapestries at the time of the Commonwealth sale he noted that the set was 'extremely well conserved, having been only used on ceremonial days'. During the 17th century the tapestries

Above: Wet cleaning a tapestry at Hampton Court. The custom-built washing machine is housed in one of the palace greenhouses.

Right: The never-ending work of tapestry conservation at Hampton Court Palace stretches back to the 1880s and the Arts & Crafts master William Morris.

Overleaf: The *Abraham* tapestries, which hang in the Great Hall, were one of the most expensive sets of tapestries commissioned by Henry VIII. The tapestries are richly woven with gilt thread and although this is now tarnished and the colours somewhat faded, they still retain much of their former splendour.

were occasionally taken up to London for state occasions. During the reign of Charles I they were hung in the Banqueting House at the signing of the peace treaty with Spain in 1630 and displayed at the receptions of the Moroccan ambassador in 1637 and the Spanish ambassador in 1640. At the coronation of James II in 1685 they provided the principal decoration in Westminster Abbey and there was a traditional association between the *Abraham* tapestries and the coronation ceremony. In the early 1700s the tapestries, which had been repaired, cleaned and given new blue and grey borders, were hung permanently for the first time when they were displayed in William III's State Apartments. In 1841 eight pieces were returned to the Great Hall while the other two were hung in the Public Dining Room before being moved to the Chapel Royal at St James's Palace. In the 1920s the set was reunited and stored in the Victoria & Albert Museum while the Great Hall was being renovated. Six pieces are now on display in the Great Hall while others are hung in the King's Apartments.

The presence of so many tapestries at Hampton Court has helped make the palace one of the world's leading centres for textile conservation and repair. In 1912 the William Morris Tapestry Company took over from the old Office of Works tapestry restorers and operated a workshop in the Queen's Guard Chamber. At the outbreak of the Second World War the company went into liquidation, and the Board of Works took the needlewomen on to the books of Hampton Court Palace, creating what came to be known for many years as the Textile Conservation Studio (now contained within Conservation and Collection Care at Historic Royal Palaces). The late 19th-century fashion for restoring tapestries and even reweaving whole sections has in recent decades been replaced by a policy of painstaking cleaning and repair. A key element of the re-presentation scheme for the State Apartments following the fire of 1986 was re-hanging tapestries that had been dispersed long before and replaced with wallpaper. The programme of cleaning and repair was described as the Textile Conservation Studio's finest hour.

The stories that every tapestry tells emerged shining and renewed.

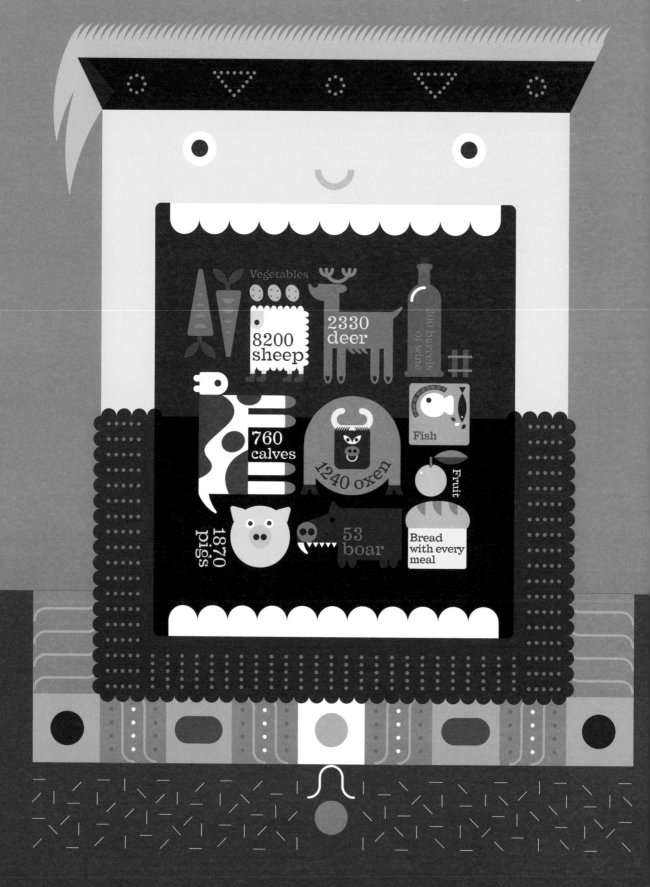

Vegetables

8200 sheep

2330 deer

300 barrels of wine

760 calves

1240 oxen

Fish

Fruit

1870 pigs

53 boar

Bread with every meal

10
Feeding the twelve hundred

Above: Henry VIII (detail) after Hans Holbein. The King ate privately in his own rooms fed from his own kitchen. Food from the Great Kitchens rarely reached the King's mouth.

Left: Meat comprised at least 75 per cent of the Tudor diet. On average a Tudor courtier would eat 4,500-5,000 calories a day (over twice the present norm) – all washed down with vast quantities of wine and ale.

When Henry VIII took over Hampton Court Palace from Cardinal Wolsey the existing kitchens were too small to feed the royal household, which could number as many as 1,200 people in the winter. As a result, in May 1529, Henry began enlarging Wolsey's Great Kitchen, a task that was completed in March 1532. Capacity was doubled. Specialised offices were each responsible for a particular part of the meal, whether boiling meat, pastry-making, storing fish or game, preparing fruits and spices; these were housed in a series of three new courtyards to the west of the existing Great Kitchen. The exception was the Bakery, which was situated outside the palace walls to minimise the risk of fire. The whole vast kitchen complex consisted of 50 rooms and three cellars. The kitchen accounts were kept by the Clerks of the Greencloth, named after the green baize-covered table at which they sat. Their office was located above the kitchen entry gate so they could monitor the supplies coming into the palace.

And all this was just to feed the court and the royal household. The King's own food was prepared elsewhere.

The majority of those at court dined in the Great Hall. As 600 were entitled to eat there and it could only house 300 people at a time there were two sittings. Senior courtiers ate in the Great Watching Chamber while the most important nobles either ate in the Council Chamber or dined in their own rooms, waited on by their own servants. In both the Great Watching Chamber and the Great Hall food was served in 'messes', large dishes containing enough food for four people. The King usually dined separately. Henry rarely ate the food that was prepared in the Great Kitchen. The King's meals were cooked in a separate Privy Kitchen located beneath his rooms, enabling him to be served the choicest morsels and allowing him greater flexibility over his meal times.

Although vegetables gained in popularity during the reign of Henry VIII, meat made up the bulk of the daily diet. In one year the Tudor court polished off more than 1,240 oxen, 8,200 sheep, 2,330 deer, 760 calves, 1,870 pigs and 53 wild boar. Meat was normally roasted on spits (seven boys were employed for the sole purpose of turning them and they were allowed extra helpings of ale to help them cool down) but was sometimes boiled. The Boiling House at Hampton Court housed an enormous 76-gallon copper cauldron with its own flight of steps to enable the cooks to stir whatever was bubbling away in it and add new joints of meat. Most Tudor food was served with sauces flavoured with spices from the Spicery. Bread, baked in small round loaves and given out from the Pantry at the west end of the Great Hall, was a major part of any meal.

The number of dishes and type of food served to a courtier depended very much on his rank and was governed by a set of rules laid down in the Household Ordinances. While household servants received four dishes at dinner, the Lord Chamberlain was entitled to sixteen, served in two courses. Only parts of the course were fully eaten. No one could possibly eat sixteen dishes and, in any case, it was considered uncharitable to finish all one's food. Leftover food was collected in a dish known as a voider and passed down to those of lesser rank. They too would pass down their leftovers. Eventually, anything remaining when everyone had eaten would be handed out to the beggars who clustered at the palace gates.

Everything was done by status. Even the type of bread eaten depended on a person's rank. The more important courtiers received manchet bread made from the best quality wheat. The rest had to make do with cheat, made from poorer quality flour. Pottage, a thick soup made with meat and thickened with cereals such as oatmeal or barley, was a commonplace part of the diet, especially for the lower courtiers. Henry VIII seems to have been particularly fond of fruit but because raw fruit was believed to cause fevers, it was usually cooked in tarts, dried or made into preserves. Although some of the meat came from the royal estates, most of the food consumed at court was bought from local farmers and markets using the ancient – and extremely unpopular – royal right of purveyance which allowed the King's agents to buy food on demand at prices below the going market rate.

Two main factors affected what was actually cooked in the kitchens: the time of year and religious observance. In the days before rapid transportation and deep-freezing, food was highly seasonal. Although animals could be kept alive to be slaughtered when required, fresh fruit and vegetables were limited to the summer months. Then the demands of religion meant that meat was never eaten during Lent or on Fridays, times of fasting, and often not on Wednesdays or Saturdays either. As a result fish was a crucial element of a courtier's diet. Saltwater fish were brought from the coast in barrels packed with seaweed while freshwater fish were kept alive in the palace ponds until needed. The ponds, although long since drained, remain as sunken gardens to the south of the palace.

By contrast, on feast days such as Christmas, Easter, Ascension and the Assumption, the variety, quality and quantity of food was increased considerably. Today the Tudor Kitchens at Hampton Court are displayed as if food is being prepared for the feast of St John the Baptist on Midsummer's Day, 1542. The menu includes roast beef, venison pie, baked carp in wine with prunes, beef with vinegar sauce, stuffed roast boar and creamed almonds. In Tudor times the centrepiece of such a meal would be a 'prodigy dish' – in this case peacock royal, a roast peacock re-dressed in its feathers. Few today will have had the chance to taste such a delicacy – opinions differ among those who have on whether it tastes good or not.

An eagerly-awaited part of any feast were sugar and almond paste confections known as 'subtleties'. These were moulded into fantastic sculptures, often of beasts or buildings and up to 3 feet (0.91 meters) high, then gilded and painted. Sugar was rare and expensive, and here was consumption at its most conspicuous.

These feasts could last for several hours. The Venetian ambassador recounted that on one occasion Henry got so bored that he passed the time by throwing sugarplums at his guests. However, this was an exception. Good table manners were expected of everyone. People washed their hands between courses, laid their napkins across their left shoulders and not on their laps and kept their elbows and fists off the table. Needless to say, at an everyday meal

The King ate in his lodging

The Lord Chamberlain

ate up to sixteen dishes

Courtiers

ate in the Great Hall

Servants

ate from the food collected in the voider

Beggars

got the leftovers

in the Great Hall with 300 hungry people waiting for their food, such social niceties were not always so strictly adhered to. According to Andrew Barclay, the Tudor poet who ate there early in Henry's reign:

> If the dish is pleasant, either flesh or fish,
> Ten hands at once swarm in the dish;
> And be it flesh, ten knives shalt thou see
> Mangling the flesh, and in the platter flee.
> To put there thy hands is peril without fail
> Without a gauntlet, or else a glove of mail.

11
'The simplest country gentlefolks'

Above: Kew Palace restored to its former glory after a comprehensive programme of research, repair and re-presentation.

Left: The bed alcove in Princess Amelia's bedroom, hastily assembled for the royal family's stay at Kew Palace in 1801.

Overleaf: Portraits of George III and Queen Charlotte by Johann Zoffany, 1771. On seeing the painting of the King at the Royal Academy, Horace Walpole commented 'Very like, but most disagreeable and unmeaning figure'. Queen Charlotte shows off the clasp of the bracelet on her right arm, decorated with a miniature portrait of her husband.

In 1751 Frederick, Prince of Wales, the eldest son of George II, died leaving a widow and their young children. The eldest was George, aged 13, who became the new Prince of Wales (later George III). He and his next brother Edward were moved into the brick-built house that is today known as Kew Palace. Then it was but one of a complex of royal houses at Kew, on the south side of the Thames down from Richmond; today it stands alone inside the Royal Botanic Gardens. This house became the princes' school, where they were taught a regular curriculum. Kew Palace carried memories of summer holidays and irregular Latin verbs.

The house was to have more painful memories too, for it was here that George was brought as a man in his late middle age suffering the ravages of an illness that bore all the signs of insanity.

The first permanent royal residence at Kew had been Richmond Lodge, a converted hunting lodge which was occupied by the future George II and his wife, Caroline. By 1729 George and Caroline had eight children, far too many for Richmond Lodge, and so their accommodation had to be supplemented by renting nearby houses. One was Kew Palace (often known as the Dutch House), built in 1631 by a successful City merchant called Samuel Fortrey. This modest house provided a residence for the King and Queen's three eldest daughters when the court was at Richmond.

In 1731 the princesses' brother, Frederick, Prince of Wales purchased a lease on a house a few hundred yards south of Kew Palace. In time this 'old timber house' as John Evelyn had described it in the previous century, was extended and refaced in Portland stone by William Kent gaining it the name the White House. This was Frederick's country residence until his early death in 1751.

Kew continued to be a favoured residence throughout most of the long reign of George III (1760-1820), partly because he had spent so much of his childhood there but also because he vigorously disliked both Hampton Court Palace and Kensington Palace. When his mother, Princess Augusta, died in 1772 and the White House became vacant, George and his wife Charlotte moved in and ordered the demolition of the old Richmond Lodge. In 1773 their two eldest sons George, Prince of Wales and Prince Frederick, then aged 11 and 10 respectively, moved into Kew Palace for their schooling just as their father had done before them.

Mrs Papendiek, Assistant Keeper of the Wardrobe to Queen Charlotte, wrote of that time:

Kew now became quite gay, the public being admitted to the Richmond Gardens on Sundays, and to Kew Gardens on Thursdays. The Green on those days was covered with carriages, more than £300 being often taken at the bridge on Sundays. Their Majesties were to be seen at the windows speaking to their friends, and the royal children amusing themselves in their own gardens. Parties came up by water too, with bands of music, to the ait [island in the Thames] opposite the Prince of Wales's house. The whole was a scene of enchantment and delight; Royalty living amongst their subjects to give pleasure and do good.

Yet Kew also afforded George III and his family privacy when they wanted it. According to one of the Queen's ladies: 'The Royal family are here always in so very retired a way, that they live as the simplest country gentlefolks. The King has not even an equerry ... nor the Queen any lady to attend her when she goes her airings'.

It was at Kew in June 1788 that George III suffered the first symptoms of porphyria, the illness that was to mar the rest of his life, when he suffered a bilious attack. By November he was exhibiting all the signs of derangement and for four months he was kept at the White House, always under supervision and sometimes under physical restraint.

Although the King recovered, there was always the prospect that the malady would recur. Twelve years later it did and he was again brought to Kew. Kew Palace was hastily made ready to receive the royal family as the White House was all but derelict. George had already embarked on a grandiose if not crazed scheme to build

Right: 'Farmer' George confronting a startled subject, as depicted by the caricaturist James Gillray in 1795.

Below: The flock of Merinos kept at Kew for the King's interest was the foundation of the Australian wool industry.

a new residence at Kew designed for him by James Wyatt in a gothic style and known as the Castellated Palace, but this was only partly completed at the time. So from 1801 until 1806, this modest merchant's house, measuring only 21 metres (70 feet) by 15 metres (50 feet) (although it originally also had a service wing which has since been demolished) was a royal palace.

On 20 April 1801 a group of doctors went to Kew in order to take control of the King. George tried to evade them when he realised their purpose but to no avail. Temporarily housed in the White House, by mid-May the King was back in Kew Palace. Within a month he was well again, but the illness returned in 1804. Once again George III was brought to Kew, where he was housed in the old service wing on the western side of Kew Palace.

The King was a devoted family man who loved his wife dearly. Sir Joshua Reynolds noted that on his return to Kew from Portsmouth in 1773 George 'was so impatient to see the Queen that he opened the chaise himself and jumped out before any of his attendants could come to his assistance. He seized the Queen, whom he met at the door, round the waist, and carried her in his arms into the room'. Throughout most of his married life the King had slept with the Queen. Now Queen Charlotte had become afraid to be alone with him owing to his attacks of 'madness'. On occasions he had become quite violent. It has been suggested that this may have been less an effect of his illness than a reaction to his treatment – he was increasingly constrained in a strait-jacket, 'the waistcoat' as he called it – but erratic violence is also a symptom of porphyria. For his own safety and that of his family the King was kept separately.

Kew had always been a place of pleasure. The gardens with their buildings and botanic rareties were among the wonders of the realm. The King kept one of his many libraries in Kew Palace. He was an avid collector of books, owning more than 65,000 volumes, most of which were housed at the Queen's House, now Buckingham Palace. (They were transferred after his death to the British Museum and can now be seen in a glass tower in the British Library at St Pancras.) It seems likely that the books he kept at Kew were those relating to his personal interests. There are books on astronomy – George built an observatory at Kew and he was a patron of Herschel – and agriculture. The King brought Merino sheep from Spain to graze at Kew, and developed a model farm on the estate for his children's instruction. When the royal family were in extended – and enforced – residence at Kew Palace, the Queen's and princesses' rooms were all redecorated in the latest fashions for their pleasure and comfort.

Although he recovered once more, by now it seemed clear that the King's illness was becoming a permanent feature. In 1806 George III left Kew for Windsor for the last time. After June 1811 he was never seen outside the walls of Windsor Castle again.

Kew Palace featured one last time in the history of the royal family. On 20 June 1818 Queen Charlotte, travelling from London to Windsor, was forced by ill health to break her journey at Kew. Her condition became grave but she lived long enough to be wheeled in to witness the marriage of two of her sons, the Dukes of Clarence and Kent, before an improvised altar in the Queen's Drawing Room. In September she told her doctor that she longed to return to Windsor,

Above: Queen Charlotte's Cottage, the royal family's picnic retreat at the southern point of Kew Gardens.

Left: The princesses' doll's house, decorated and furnished much as the palace would have been in the early 19th century.

'but I am very weak'. On 17 November 1818 she died in her bedchamber at Kew Palace, holding the hand of her eldest son, the Prince of Wales. King George, who by now was senile, blind and deaf, was quite unaware that his beloved wife had gone. He died himself fourteen months later.

George's great building project at Kew also ended in failure. When work began on the Castellated Palace in 1801 the original estimate of the cost of building it was £40,000. Ten years later £500,000 had been spent and it was still only half-finished. In the end Parliament, increasingly unhappy at the spiralling costs, condemned the building. In 1828 the Select Committee on Public Accounts, hoping to rescue something from this financial and architectural fiasco, directed that the place should be demolished and the materials re-used on other royal palaces. St James's Palace, Windsor Castle and Buckingham Palace were all allocated a quota of materials. An old king's dreams lay in ruins.

The diminutive and domestic Kew Palace is what remains, a repository for stories of enchantment and illness, royal childhoods and royal despair.

12

'Fortifications which the French call castles'

William the Conqueror clashes with King Harold II at the Battle of Hastings. After his victory, William rewarded many of his supporters with land confiscated from the Anglo-Saxon nobility. Within a generation, the Normans had built over 500 castles across the country.

1066 is supposed to be the date that everyone can remember, the year of the Norman Conquest. Leading a relatively small band of warriors from Normandy, William the Conqueror took power from the Anglo-Saxon rulers and imposed a new order. William I's conquest of England has sometimes been described as swift and effective but, although it was ultimately effective, it was anything but swift. The story of the conquest is intertwined with the story of one of its most visible and enduring monumental symbols: the Tower of London.

Defeat at Hastings on 14 October 1066 cost the English their best chance of repelling the Norman invasion, deprived them of their most effective leaders and handed the strategic initiative to William. Yet it would still take the Conqueror nearly five years of hard, brutal campaigning to establish control over England. He was faced with a hostile population, periodic rebellion, Welsh and Viking raiding parties and, towards the end of his reign, the real threat of a Scandinavian invasion. Perhaps 10,000 Normans subdued a population of 2 million, an army of occupation that lived, ate and slept in strongholds from which a few men could dominate a hostile population.

William had fought at Hastings because he had to – he needed to defeat Harold before too many troops could join the English King, Harold Godwinson. Normally William avoided pitched battles, preferring instead to bring an area to its knees by ravaging it. The most graphic example of his strategy is the 'Harrying of the North', the systematic devastation of the north of England during the harsh winter of 1069-70 in response to three rebellions in two years. The bulk of the population of northern England either died or became refugees. By 1086, when the great Domesday Book record of landholding was compiled, there were only four major landholders of English birth left. All the others were Normans who had seized land and title.

In these circumstances, the widespread construction of castles was to be a major factor in the Normans' ability to conquer and hold the country. Castles served as bases for military operations, as refuges in the event of rebellion, as administrative centres and as novel, powerful symbols of Norman dominance. A 12th-century chronicler commented, 'in the lands of the English there were very few of those fortifications which the French call castles; in consequence the English, for all their martial qualities and valour, were at a disadvantage when it came to resisting their enemies'.

Once William had defeated the English at Hastings he knew that he had to secure London, the kingdom's richest and most populous city. He avoided attacking it directly. Instead he marched westwards, ravaging and burning as he went before crossing the Thames at Wallingford, circling round the Chilterns to reach Little Berkhamsted in Hertfordshire. There the magnates of London came out to meet him, surrendered the city and offered him the crown. According to the chronicler William of Poitiers, William then 'sent men ahead into London to build a fortress' and, a few days later, his troops

entered London. On Christmas Day 1066, William was crowned in Westminster Abbey (which has been the English coronation church ever since). It is reported that, on hearing some English shouts of acclamation outside the abbey, William's troops thought that a riot had broken out and responded by setting fire to neighbouring houses. The ceremonies continued amidst the smoke and commotion, with William trembling like a leaf. Then, aware of the 'inconstancy of the numerous and hostile inhabitants', he left London 'while fortifications were being completed'.

While William founded more than one castle in the city – others were constructed in the areas now known as Blackfriars and Ludgate Circus – the future Tower of London would quickly become the most important.

Many of the castles built in England by the Normans were of the 'motte and bailey' type: a mound with a wooden tower surrounded by a stockade and ditch. Occasionally, however, the Normans would adapt existing fortifications for their purposes. In choosing the site for their main castle in London, the Normans took advantage of the ready-made defences provided by the right-angled bend in the south-east corner of the ancient Roman city walls. By demolishing the houses of those inhabitants unfortunate enough to be living in the area and fortifying its other two sides with a ditch and an earth and timber rampart, the Normans created an enclosure. It contained lodgings, storehouses, stables and, soon, the enormous structure that came to be known as the White Tower.

Above: Building the White Tower in the 1070s, which was made of French stone to remind us who was boss!

Right: William, Duke of Normandy in a detail from the Bayeux Tapestry, which celebrated the conquest of England.

Far right: The tranquil Chapel of St John the Evangelist in the White Tower – one of the most important church interiors of its date in England.

Overleaf: The White Tower, enduring symbol of the Conqueror's power.

A few Norman castle towers were built from stone from the start, notably Colchester in Essex and Richmond in Yorkshire. The White Tower was one of these. Measuring 36 metres (118 feet) by 32.5 metres (107 feet) and standing over 27 metres (88 feet) tall, it is one of the largest structures of its type ever built (and second only in size to the great castle keep at Colchester, Essex). This imposing symbol of conquest, power and might was not even constructed from English materials. The stone was brought from Caen in Normandy (the city in which the Conqueror is buried) as a further reminder of who was boss.

Today, the building consists of four levels, each divided into three main parts: a large room on the west side, a smaller one to the east and the chapel and the spaces below it in the south-east corner. The lowest level, half-underground, lit by small slits and with no external entrance, was probably conceived as a storage area although it did house the castle well. The main entrance was on the floor above, reached by a timber staircase which ran along the south wall. Both this level and the one above were equipped with fireplaces and latrines. The top floor of the tower was only inserted in the 15th century and the marks of the original roof can still be seen on the walls there. A contemporary document states that Gundulf, Bishop of Rochester and one of the great builders of his age, supervised 'the king's works on the great tower of London'. Gundulf was made Bishop in 1077 and this has been taken to suggest that work on the tower was begun at this time. However, Gundulf may have been working on the tower before he was appointed bishop, and building may well have been underway before he became involved in the project. The tower was an early element in the Conqueror's bid for control.

The White Tower (which takes its name from the fact that, in common with many other castles of the period, it was whitewashed in the 13th century) had an obvious military function. It dominated the potentially hostile city of London, would have provided a virtually impregnable refuge in the event of rebellion and commanded the approach to London up the River Thames. However, this was not the White Tower's only function. For over a century before the Norman Conquest, the kings and lords of France had been building towers in their main towns to serve not only as fortresses and demonstrations of their owners' wealth and power but also as residences. William's great grandfather, Duke Richard of Normandy had constructed two in Bayeux and Rouen. The White Tower may be seen as coming from that tradition. Indeed its design may well have been based on a similar tower at Ivry-la-Bataille, near Evreux in Normandy.

The sheer scale of the building, the magnificence of its chapel and the inclusion of domestic features such as latrines and fireplaces (possibly the earliest in England), confirm that the White Tower was always intended to have a major peacetime role as a royal residence in the capital city. The King possibly used the slightly more luxurious accommodation on the second floor and his Constable the rooms on the floor below. This extraordinary building is, therefore, not just a powerful and enduring symbol of the Norman Conquest – it is England's first great royal palace.

✳

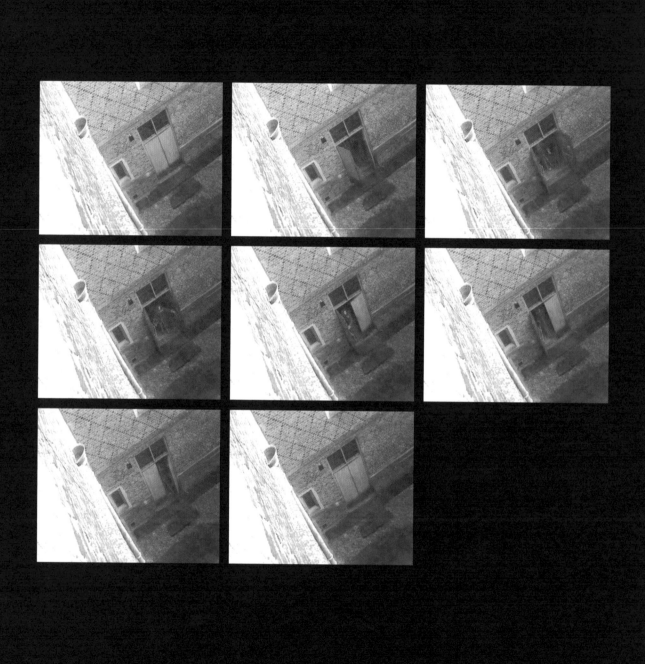

13
Everything but the ghost

Above: A Victorian shocker. Queen Catherine Howard and her executioner stalk the palace, as captured by trick photography.

Left: Star of CCTV – 'Skeletor' captured on camera in 2004 and the newest addition to Hampton Court Palace's complement of ghosts.

Hampton Court. Hallowe'en. Their hearts pounding, two women walk nervously through the half light of the palace's infamous Haunted Gallery, where the ghost of Catherine Howard, the fifth wife of Henry VIII, is said to run in a vain attempt to reach the King and plead for her life. As they reach the end of the gallery a shadowy figure moves towards them … It's State Apartment Warder, Ian Franklin, their guide on tonight's ghost tour.

While the tours visit a variety of sites at Hampton Court Palace, each with a ghostly story, the opportunity to walk in pairs down what is reputedly the most haunted part of the palace is the highlight of the evening for many participants. Indeed, it has all been a bit much for some. During separate evening tours of the palace in 1999, two female visitors fainted on exactly the same spot and on a more recent tour two distinguished historians reported feeling an icy coldness surround them as they stood together in the gallery. Ian has long been fascinated by the many tales of ghostly sightings and eerie experiences associated with the palace and has delved deeply into both the stories and the history surrounding them. Like all the guides who conduct the ghost tours, Ian presents the facts and then lets people make up their own minds. Was that ghostly sighting merely the reflection of a security guard's torch? Could the sighting of two phantom cavaliers be explained by the discovery of a pair of bodies in a shallow grave in the 1870s? Who is the mysterious cloaked figure filmed opening a fire door on the palace's CCTV? Whatever one's views on ghosts, what cannot be denied is the fact that many perfectly rational people – staff and visitors alike – have experienced strange phenomena for which there is often no obvious explanation.

It is interesting to note that a recent investigation carried out by a team from the University of Hertfordshire claimed to have identified two unusual 'cold spots' in the Haunted Gallery, caused by concealed doors. These 'ghostbusters', as the papers delighted in calling them, suggested that this sudden drop in temperature could be attributed by some to a ghostly encounter. They also argued that other 'normal' environmental factors such as differences in lighting levels and changes in local magnetic fields may be unconsciously interpreted as evidence of ghostly activity.

So there is a rational explanation after all … Or is there? Come along on a ghost tour and make up your own mind.

Ian Franklin, State Apartment Warder

she laid her
head down upon
the block, and
stretched forth
her body and said:
'*Lord, into thy
hands I commend
my spirit!*'
And so she ended.

14
'Dispatch me quickly'

Lady Jane Grey by William James Grant, late 19th century. The graffiti depicted still survives today.

Nothing in the short life of Jane Grey, who was queen for but nine days in 1553, was quite as magnificent as her composure in facing death:

His [her husband Dudley's] carcase thrown into a cart, and his head in a cloth, he was brought to the chapel within the Tower, where the Lady Jane, whose lodging was in Partridge's house, did see his dead carcase taken out of the cart, as well as she did see him before alive on going to his death – a sight to her no less than death. By this time there was a scaffold made upon the green over against the White Tower, for the said lady Jane to die upon … The said lady, being nothing abashed … prayed all the way till she came to the said scaffold … Then the hangman kneeled down, and asked her forgiveness, whom she gave most willingly. Then he willed her to stand upon the straw: which doing, she saw the block. Then she said, 'I pray you dispatch me quickly.' Then she kneeled down … She tied the kercher about her eyes; then feeling for the block said, 'What shall I do? Where is it?' One of the standers-by guiding her thereto, she laid her head down upon the block, and stretched forth her body and said: 'Lord, into thy hands I commend my spirit!' And so she ended.

Despite its grim reputation as a place of torture and death, the Tower of London was usually no more than a point of departure for prisoners led off for execution elsewhere, normally at Tower Hill and then later Tyburn (where Marble Arch stands today). The 'privilege' of being executed in the relative privacy of the Tower was normally only given to those of particularly high rank or else to people whose popularity might make a public execution too dangerous. As a result, with the exception of a handful of executions during the two World Wars, only seven people were actually executed within the walls of the Tower itself. Even so, three queens were to lose their heads there in the space of only eighteen years: Anne Boleyn, Catherine Howard and Jane Grey.

Anne Boleyn had married Henry VIII in 1533 and was crowned queen in May, but by 1536 she had fallen from the King's favour, after giving birth to a daughter, Elizabeth, and then miscarrying a boy. When Henry had fallen in love with Anne he hoped that she would be able to provide him with the male heir that he craved and that his first wife, Catherine of Aragon, had been unable to do. The consequences of Henry's struggle to divorce Catherine and marry Anne remain with us to this day.

By now Henry had fallen in love again, with Jane Seymour, one of Anne's Ladies-in-Waiting, and he was beginning to listen to conservative intrigue against Anne, who was a supporter of Protestant religious reform. In April she was arrested on trumped-up charges of treason: adultery, incest and plotting to murder the King. On 15 May, Anne and her brother, Lord Rochford, were tried before their peers in the Great Hall of the Tower, which had been repaired for her coronation only three years before. Despite their protestations of innocence, they were condemned to die.

Tradition has it that Anne was then moved to two rooms on the first floor of the Lieutenant's lodgings opposite Tower Green, now known as the Queen's House. In fact the Queen's House was not built until four years after her death. She was actually lodged in the old palace in the Tower, most of which has since been demolished. On 17 May her supposed lovers were executed on Tower Hill and two days later, at eight o'clock in the morning, she stepped on to the scaffold that had been built on Tower Green. The executioner from Calais, an expert who used a sword instead of an axe, had been brought across the Channel to carry out the sentence. According to an observer, 'she kneeled down on both her knees, and said, "To Jesus Christ I commend my soul" and with that word suddenly the hangman of Calais smote off her head at one stroke with a sword: her body with the head was buried in the choir of the Chapel in the Tower'.

That very night Henry dined with Jane Seymour and their betrothal took place the following day. Within two weeks the pair were married and workmen were being paid overtime for removing Anne's badges and initials from Hampton Court Palace and replacing them with those of Jane Seymour. Within a short space of time Jane would be dead and the workmen would be hard at work again changing the palace as three further women moved in and out of the King's bed and affections.

The niece of the Duke of Norfolk, Catherine Howard was promoted by the conservative faction in Henry's court to console him after the fiasco of his marriage to Anne of Cleves, Jane's successor as Henry's consort. Henry was delighted with his new young bride whom he married in 1540. Catherine was not the blushing virgin that she seemed but a flirtatious young woman who had been unchaste before her marriage and possibly unfaithful after it. She was in a potentially adulterous liaison with Thomas Culpepper, one of Henry's Gentlemen of the Bedchamber, with the connivance of Lady Rochford, her Lady-in-Waiting. When evidence of Catherine's indiscretions reached him, the politically scheming Archbishop of Canterbury, Thomas Cranmer, saw an opportunity to weaken the power of his opponents at court and passed the information on to the King at once. He put the accusations in a letter placed on the King's chair for Henry to find when he heard Mass in the Chapel Royal of Hampton Court Palace.

A humiliated and grief-stricken Henry turned viciously against Catherine. She was accused of leading 'an abominable, base, carnal, voluptuous, and vicious life, like a common harlot, with diverse persons'. Before being sent down the Thames to Syon Abbey to await her fate, Catherine was held under house arrest in her lodgings at Hampton Court. The story goes that she managed to escape from her rooms and run along what is now known as the Haunted Gallery in a bid to reach Henry who was praying in the Chapel and to plead for her life. Just before she reached the door she was seized by her guards, who dragged her back, screaming, to her rooms.

In truth there is no contemporary evidence for this event – and Catherine would not have been able to reach the Haunted Gallery from her rooms in any case. This has not prevented repeated sightings over the years of a ghostly female figure running screaming along the gallery towards the Chapel door.

Previous: *The Execution of Lady Jane Grey* by Paul Delaroche, 1833. By transferring the action from Tower Green to a gloomy crypt, Delaroche creates one of the most powerful images of the Tower's bloody history.

Above: *Anne Boleyn in the Tower* (detail) by Edouard Cibot, 1835. Shortly before her death, the Queen wrote in her prayer book 'Remember me when you do pray, that hope doth lead from day to day.'

Above right: Catherine Howard by Hans Holbein the Younger. According to the French ambassador, by the time of her execution Catherine was 'so weak that she could hardly speak'.

On 1 December 1541 both Culpepper and Dereham, Catherine's former lover, were arraigned for treason and condemned to die; nine days later they were both beheaded. In February 1542 an Act of Attainder was passed against Catherine, sentencing her to death for treason. When the lords of the Council arrived at Syon to escort her to the Tower of London, she became hysterical and had to be manhandled into the waiting barge. In the Tower, however, she seems to have recovered her composure a little and is said to have asked for the execution block to be brought to her room so that she could practise kneeling before it. On 13 February 1542 she was beheaded with an axe on Tower Green and buried near Anne Boleyn in the Chapel of St Peter ad Vincula. Lady Rochford, her Lady-in-Waiting, shared her fate.

The last of the three queens was Jane Grey, who was a great-niece of Henry VIII through her mother, the Duchess of Suffolk. In 1553 she was married to Guildford Dudley, the son of the Duke of Northumberland, as part of a scheme hatched by Northumberland and the dying Edward VI to prevent Princess Mary, a Catholic and Edward's half-sister, from succeeding to the throne. On 6 July 1553 Edward died and Jane was duly proclaimed queen. Although the majority of England's leading politicians backed Jane's succession, the country as a whole was outraged by the exclusion of Henry's daughters. A series of provincial uprisings broke out and Northumberland's regime collapsed within a fortnight. Mary acceded to the throne on 3 August and Northumberland was executed nineteen days later.

Mary knew full well that Jane had been an innocent puppet in the whole affair and initially spared her life, but after Sir Thomas Wyatt's Protestant rebellion of early 1554 came near to toppling her, Mary reluctantly concluded that the 17-year-old girl and her young husband had to die. On 12 February 1554 the pair were beheaded. The barbarism of the event is tempered by the dignity and composure that Jane exhibited that day.

15
A job not to be sneezed at

The Grinling Gibbons' carvings at Kensington Palace are cleaned every six months, a task that takes two conservators seven hours to complete.

Fibres from clothes, carpets and furnishings, skin flakes, human and animal hair, insect body parts and faeces, soil, pollen, gravel, glass, brick and plaster. Put them together and what have you got? Dust! Tiny fragments of all these materials have been found in the dust carried into the buildings of Historic Royal Palaces on bodies and feet, and through windows and doors as particles suspended in the air. Indeed, with 120 rooms filled with historic objects, most on open display, and over 1 kilometre (0.62 miles) of gilded picture frames, the palaces could well be described as one of the country's biggest dust traps. As Kerren Harris, Preventive Conservator for Historic Royal Palaces explains, dust is not only unsightly but also encourages pests, can seriously damage an item through its acidity and, if it is left on a surface for too long, can become cemented to it and impossible to remove.

As a result, ten preventive conservators are deployed across four historic sites in the constant battle against dust, working to a complicated cleaning schedule. Each object on display has a project sheet detailing how often it needs to be dusted. This could vary from once every six months for a chandelier to every other day for the console tables in the Teck Saloon at Kensington Palace.

Work normally begins at about 8.30am so that items in visitor circulation areas can be attended to before the palaces open to the public. At ten o'clock the conservators move to work in roped-off areas. The nature of their duties means that they come into daily contact with visitors and are asked a wide variety of questions ranging from enquiries about the objects on display to requests for tips on cleaning and dusting at home. It is clear that the conservators are ideally placed to help explain the work of Historic Royal Palaces to visitors and this was recognised by the innovative 'Ask the Conservator' scheme, which ran at Kensington Palace and Hampton Court Palace in November 2005. It was so successful that it has now become permanent. But the battle against dust still goes on!

Kerren Harris, Preventive Conservator

Acknowledgements

Published by
Historic Royal Palaces
Hampton Court Palace
Surrey
KT8 9AU

© Historic Royal Palaces, 2006
Reprinted 2015

All rights reserved. No part of this publication may be
reproduced or transmitted in any form or by any means
electronic or mechanical, including photocopying,
recording or any information storage and retrieval system,
without permission in writing from the publisher.

ISBN 978-1-873993-07-1

Edited by David Souden and Clare Murphy
Designed by Wolff Olins
Colonel Blood illustrations by Bill Bragg
Tudor Kitchens illustrations by Grundy & Northedge
Printed by BKT Ltd.

Illustrations

© The Board of Trustees of the Armouries: pages 26, 28, 30;
British Library, London, UK/Bridgeman Art Library: page 65;
© Copyright The British Museum: page 61 (BMC 8616); City of
London, London Metropolitan Archives: page 31; By Permission
of Lord Dalmeny: pages 36-37; Ian Franklin Collection: page 13;
© Guildhall Library, City of London/Bridgeman Art Library: page
29 (top); Crown copyright: Historic Royal Palaces: pages 14,
16, 21, 22-23, 24, 29 (bottom), 32, 65, 66 (drawing: Ivan Lapper),
67 (right); © Historic Royal Palaces: pages 6, 7, 8, 9, 10-11,
36, 39, 48, 52, 54-55, 60-61, 70, 71; © Historic Royal Palaces.
Photograph: Nick Guttridge: pages 35, 38, 45, 56, 57; © Historic
Royal Palaces. Photograph: Robin Forster: pages 18, 25, 50-51,
52, 78; © Historic Royal Palaces. Photograph: Julian Anderson:
pages 68-69; © Historic Royal Palaces/newsteam.co.uk.
Photograph: Richard Lea-Hair: page 44; © Historic Royal Palaces
/newsteam.co.uk. Photograph: Shaun Fellows: page 17; Hulton
Archive/Getty Images: page 15; Edward Impey: page 27;
London's Transport Museum: page 12; Musée de la Tapisserie,
Bayeux, France/Bridgeman Art Library: page 67 (left); Musée
Rolin, Autun, France/Bridgeman Art Library: page 76-77;
Courtesy of the Museum of London: page 43; © National Gallery,
London: pages 74-75; © Crown copyright. NMR: page 49; National
Museums Liverpool (The Walker): page 53; Photo: National
Portrait Gallery, London: page 73; Mick Rock: page 33; The Royal
Collection © 2006 Her Majesty Queen Elizabeth II: pages 20, 34,
40, 41, 42, 46, 47, 58, 59, 77.

Historic Royal Palaces is a registered charity (no. 1068852)